The Curious Courtship of Women's Liberation and Socialism

by
Batya Weinbaum

South End Press

I am grateful for permission to quote from Karl Marx, *Capital,* Volume I, International Publishers; Betty Friedan, *It Changed My Life,* Random House; Ellen Wright for conversations with Simone de Beauvoir; and Angelica Balabanoff, *My Impressions of Lenin,* University of Michigan Press.

Cover design by Rebecca Schiffrin
Library of Congress Catalog Card No: 77-9240
ISBN 0-89608-045-5
ISBN 0-89608-046-3

Printed by Maple Vail, York, PA., U.S.A.

Typesetting and paste up done by the collective at:
**South End Press, Box 68, Astor Station
Boston, MA 02123**

DEDICATION

This excessive fear of judgement. I am judged. I am rejected; told I can't communicate, that I am wrong. Then why can't I think of it as a bingo game? Or baseball? You get up there; nine times out of ten you get struck out because the other guy is aiming; then every once in awhile, you hit a home run!"

—journal   July, 1977

I dedicate this book to Dale Bernstein, for systematically assisting me in getting to know my own mind.

ACKNOWLEDGEMENTS

I wish to thank Monique Appollon for typing; Constance Blake, Lizzie Borden and Billy Pope for copyediting; Sheila Collins, Barbara Ehrenreich and Rayna Reiter for helping me to raise funds; Cornelia Brunner, Annie Chamberlin, Lucy Gilbert, Deborah Herst, Ruby Rorlich-Leavitt and Paula Webster for participating in a monthly discussion and support group while I struggled to write this book; the women of Theology of the Americas and Union of Radical Political Economics for sustained interest in my work; the *Review of Radical Political Economics* for excerpting an earlier version; the Rabinowitz Foundation and the Robins Flemming Fund for responding to my appeal for grants; Janet Salaff for reading the finished pre-proof version; and the members of the Sea Gate Villa community for welcoming me to their congenial atmosphere which I found most conducive to writing.

"What are you holding, a gun?" she asked as I strolled back up to the row of bungalow shacks along Coney Island behind the boardwalk. No, actually, first she asked me if I had bad feet. I said, "No, why?" She pointed to my hands, palms down on my blue thighs. I said I had a gun. If only she knew what I held inside, I said to myself; I told her I needed to protect myself on the beach. "Yes, it's fearful," she said, nodding her silvering head against the back of her rickety rocking chair. I ambled into my pink rented room, taken for the summer to finish the last-five-years' project. I put water on the little gas range for the coffee. I settled down, laughing at all my glaring posters: 5" x 8" pink and blue index cards gashed in green magic marker DAVID AND CHRIS TOOK A COURSE AT BOSTON PSYCHOANALY-TIC...MIKE NICHOLS SAID YAH, WHAT THE HELL...PAULA SAID SHE WOULD READ THIS

BEFORE SHE LEFT...WHAT ELSE CAN I DO EXCEPT STEP OUTSIDE OF HISTORY AND ADMIT WHAT I KNOW...CAPITALISM'S SUBVERSION OF PATRIARCHY FOR THE MAJORITY OF FATHERS PROVOKES SOCIALIST REACTION TO GAINS MADE BY WOMEN

I imagined on the beach after relishing a joint on the lifeguardchair that I succeeded in structuring this book unconsciously, like I did my novel. The text is constantly planting questions, dropping ideas in people's minds, urging them to pick up dropped pieces after they continue on. It's sort of a gentle prodder. It forces people to participate, recall again, in their own minds, pick up and bring together the dropped threads. That's what theory building is like. Freud did it. Bergson talked about the creative function of the mind, constantly refocusing again on itself, with the same critical eye that saw the exterior's missing pieces. Look how Bergson—a man I don't know, long since dead, who if we had met would have spoken in another language—has become an intimate part of me. Look how I remember what other people write, what other people have said— and so they take me inside them. It is, yes, an intimate, interior connection. Thank god for print.

But I was writing of the beach. The people here became very interested in encouraging me with my writing today. Even a little hare-lipped girl came in. And Charley. The one-armed retired policeman who is always drunk and sometimes wears a blond woman's wig. He came to swim by me on the ocean. Jimmy, the proprietor, smiled, as did Frank, the fellah who will some day, when he is sober, teach me how to play horseshoes, as he is the champ. A man among men. They all wanted to know why I was furiously typing. I said, "A deadline!!" They said, "You can make it! Carry on!!"

Encouragement to communicate with the living. Even with the deformed.

Angelica, Alexandra, Rosa, Clara, for you, I will carry on!

Does it mean do everything we can to liberate women and provoke the socialist revolution in reaction to ourselves? By our own conscious intention? Or does it mean be good and make socialism come first, because capitalism is really awful? Nah—leave that to the men. Call it a division of labor.

But please, go on. You will notice a change in the style of writing as I move from the uncomfortable position of belligerent critic to the experience of conceptualizing a brand new theory.

I have succeeded. I have made sense of everything I know.

Table of Contents

Part One

Part Two

Part Three

PART ONE

Chapter One

The Importance of the Concept of Revolution

Excerpts from a dialogue with Simone de Beauvoir, by Betty Friedan, in *It Changed my Life*, Random House, 1976:

Friedan: I thought it might be important for us to have a dialogue now for this reason: the women's movement, which I think we both have helped to influence by our books and through our thinking, has emerged as the largest and fastest growing—perhaps the only vital—movement for basic social change in the seventies. But it has reached in America, and to some extent, in the world, a kind of crest, and now it is floundering a little on a plateau...

3

de Beauvoir: I don't think at all that the Communist or Socialist systems as they are practiced answer this need. But I think there is a very strong relationship between the economic struggle and the feminist movement... There are feminists who are concerned only with what you are talking about: the revolt against men, lesbianism, and so on, but there are many others involved with the socialist movements, who try to connect the sex struggle with the economic class struggle and try to work with the women workers....

Friedan: I have been putting together an economic think tank for women and one of the questions is how to put a minimum wage value on housework. This could be recognized for Social Security, for pensions, and in the division of property if there is a divorce. Surely the poor and the middle-class housewife would identify with that.

de Beauvoir: There I don't agree at all. It makes for a segregation; it puts the woman in the house even more. I and my friends in the MLF don't agree with that at all. It's keeping to the idea of women de Beauvoir: at home, and I'm very much against it... We think that every individual, woman as well as man, should work outside and have the possibility, either by communal living, collectives, or another way of organizing the family, of solving the problems of day care. Not keep the same system of creches, but change the system so that the choices available are different. Something along these lines is being tried in China. For example, on a certain day in the community, everyone—men, women, and children, as far as they are capable—come together to do all the washing and darning of socks...

Friedan: Are we talking about society today or about some remote future? In some of the Communist countries, instead of restructuring the jobs to take maternity into account, it has been decided to pay the women to stay at home and pay the men more to keep the women home. I think this is a reactionary move.

From Barbara Ehrenreich's speech at the National Socialist/Feminist Conference, July, 1975, reprinted in *WIN,* June 3, 1976:

> To discuss a socialist country such as China as a patriarchy—as I have heard radical feminists do—is to ignore the real struggles and achievements of millions of women. Socialist feminists, while agreeing that there is something timeless and universal about women's oppression, have insisted it takes different forms in different settings, and that the *differences* are of vital importance. There is a difference between a society in which sexism is expressed in the form of female infanticide and a society in which sexism takes the form of unequal representation on the Central Committee. And the difference is worth dying for.

It seems to me that a country that
wiped out the tse tse fly can by fiat
put an equal number of women on
the Central Committee.

"Notes of an ex-China Fan,"
Susan Brownmiller, *Village Voice.*

The question of revolution, by giving shape to
the analysis we use and, to a large extent, by determining how we group ourselves for action, ranks as
an important question in a movement among women. I mean this both in the immediate sense of
choice of tactics considered appropriate and in the
longer perspective of historical development. I say
this because I have noticed how, ever since the existing socialist societies have dawned on this earth,
disillusionment with socialism, which results from
revolution, has been an impetus to the emergence of
feminist theory. Think how disillusionment with
contemporary revolutionary movements has helped
to spawn feminists here. Marge Piercy's essay, "The
Grand Coolie Damn," published in *Leviathan,* one of
the first women's liberation journals in the U.S., is
but an incident in this dialectical process. "The
movement is supposed to be for human liberation:
how come the condition of women inside it is no

better than on the outside?" she asked in 1969.[1] It seems that until such shortcomings of both revolutionary result and means manifest themselves, motivation for new theoretic formulation lags behind the need for solace to be taken from the undefined future—in the face of an overwhelmingly depressing (since oppressing) capitalist present. We find it easier and more comforting to put off the "woman question" in the hope that though sexism might be bad now, after the revolution, somehow, it all gets better. For nearly a hundred years this vague faith in the post-revolutionary era has been the rationale for positions taken by women in the left. Starting with Clara Zetkin and the Second International in Europe, this "after the revolution" trust has been eulogized, much as belief in the next world or the afterlife seems to operate for those with more traditional religious convictions. The same force of conviction, it might be argued, underlies the appeal of small measures taken in socialist countries, such as the collective sock-darning and clothes-washing mentioned by Simone de Beauvoir in her dialogue with Betty Friedan. Yet, the Marxist notion of revolution, and not an overall vision of feminist revolution, has been the concept motivating change in these societies; consequently, with every tarnish on the brilliance of an expected socialist future, we are forced to clarify our own concept of *feminist* revolution.

In this respect, breakthroughs in feminist thinking parallel further refinements in socialist thinking which occur in a similar manner at the same time. It is worthwhile to note, for example, that de Beauvoir wrote *The Second Sex,* a path breaking exploration of women's oppression, as disillusionment with the Soviet Union spread in post-war European intellectual circles.[2] In her novel *The Mandarins* her own experience of this process might be surmised; she critiques her male comrades of the era much as we heard Marge Piercy express her own decade's voice.[3] In the more subtle French fashion, de Beauvoir writes of a leading left intellectual who has an affair with an ex-Nazi mistress, the coquettish star in one of his plays. This strikes me as a perfect symbol of what must have been extreme depression. For it was a time when many leftists, shocked by discoveries of the Soviet labor camps after the war, had had their fill of the illicit links between socialism and fascism. Since the time when Stalin made a pact with Hitler, discomfort with the behind-the-scenes ties between the two supposedly different systems had been brewing; finally a critique of the "social fascist" nature of the Soviet Union began to take hold.

There is yet another similarity in the process of the development of the two movements which until recently have largely been considered separately. That is, as it might be expected, critiques of existing socialist societies tend to reflect the concerns of the criticizers. I say this might be expected, as one's thinking is shaped fundamentally by grappling with the problems experienced in one's own society. From the experience leading up to and following World War II, Western Europeans were primarily concerned with the problem of fascism. This concern was reflected, not only in the "social fascist" concept I mentioned before, but also in the critiques of Soviet society generated by those who found refuge in the United States, and focused on psychoanalytic bases for authoritarianism and repression, such as Marcuse, or totalitarianism, such as Hannah Arendt.[4] In the historical era in which we now live, on the other hand, the major capitalist countries recently experienced a protest movement provoked by the war in Vietnam. A generation, so radicalized, produced critiques of existing socialist countries which emphasize the imperialist nature of those economic systems. Much as the U.S. exploits the resource base of Third World countries, it has been argued, the Soviet Union exploits the economic base of its Eastern European satellites and Cuba. This critique has been elaborated, as our own government's role in engineering the 1973 military coup which overthrew the Chilean socialist government has become a source of protest. American leftists expressed indignation with China's immediate recognition of the fascist dictatorship which had taken charge over the Chilean people. As our foreign policy was the major issue here, foreign policy of socialist countries came under the critical spotlight.

Why go to such lengths to observe similarities in the timing and process of socialist and feminist theoretical development? Because so often feminists are accused by socialists of projecting American feminist concerns onto other cultures. This might be true, yet since awareness of oneself is magnified by examination of the *other,* the accusation seems more like a dodge than a charge warranting dismissal. Perhaps I differ from others in thinking that critiques of socialisms *should* project domestic dilemmas, so that if American feminism is developing a

notion of patriarchy, then we should see how socialism both is and is not a patriarchy; and that if
European leftists are fighting fascism, then they
should see how socialism does and does not counteract fascistic components of society; and that if in the
course of a movement against U.S. imperialism,
leftists are created, then those leftists should see how
socialism is and is not imperialistic; but I have good
reason to differ. To fancy that the intellect dominates over psychologically-projected constructs is to
delude oneself about the power of rationality, in the
first place; and, moreover, to engage in debates over
"what went wrong" in the socialisms we know today
is only valuable insofar as it serves precisely such a
political Rorschach purpose. For by concretizing our
actual disappointments with the post-revolutionary
after-life, our understanding of what bothers us in
the still-capitalist environment can only become
more specific. And specificity enhances our facility
to enlarge upon the concept of revolution, which
theoretically guides our actions day by day, just as
the concept of an after-life posed by a religious
doctrine determines the morality lived in every
waking day by its followers. That waking day is different for the devout Methodist, the Orthodox Jew,
the fundamentalist Baptist, for each is preparing
according to a different expectation of a proper
death.

Marx and Engels referred to socialism in the
Communist Manifesto, in *Socialism: Utopian or
Scientific,* and throughout the whole of their writing, in just such a vein of practicality.[5] By appealing
to the possibility of a radically different future, not in
death, but attainable by mortal beings, they criti-

cized the politics of those with whom they differed: this tactic, this approach, this way of thinking, they protested, will not help us arrive at the threshold of the new society which we want and which we think is attainable. And many were attracted by the power of the vision they projected. That creative quality of imaginative evocation has largely been lost since socialist societies have come into existence. Instead, the tendency has been to substitute factual information drawn from existing socialist societies. Among socialists this tendency induces a reliance on what is already known and so constricts the emergence of new thinking; among the audience of socialists the tendency induces a passive absorption of information, just as students are taught to learn in the schools. Don't we criticize this process? For it hardly engages the mind in a gripping endeavour. The mind can easily respond with counter-information, the supply of which is vast. The socialists then respond by saying, "That's not socialism anyway," after a certain period of history, and we go back to ground one: the need for a vision of what *might* come if we refine our tactics.

By discerning which constituent parts remain operative when Marx's visionary concept of revolution gets put into practice, we take a rare opportunity to see beyond the Marxist given with which socialists tend to answer the "woman question." Our question then becomes, not, "how do women fit into the revolution," but, "what kind of revolution do women need?" Can we first separate the Marxist and feminist criteria for change, recombine them, and finally, in the new juxtaposition, discover a more satisfying solution?

It is my opinion that in the end the risk of temporarily antagonistic dichotomization is worth the gain. For the emerging synthesis will create a space for a vision of the kind of society we would like to develop. And I feel we are in need of that vision. Juliet Mitchell, one of the first Marxist-feminist writers, commented in 1971 that the theoretical impasse between Marxism and Feminism seemed to stem from the abstract nature of the debates. It seemed, she wrote in *Women's Estate,* that these debates were not based on anything so tangible as practice.[6] By focusing on the practical aspects of theory—the vision of change or revolution—I attempt to move us on.

Footnotes

1. Marge Piercy, *Leviathan,* Nov. 1969, and now available from New England Free Press in pamphlet form.
2. Simone de Beauvoir, *The Second Sex,* Vintage, New York, 1974.
3. Simone de Beauvoir, *The Mandarins,* World Publishing Co. Cleveland, 1956, and Piercy *op. cit.,* 1969.
4. Herbert Marcuse, *Soviet Marxism,* Vintage Books, New York, 1971; and Hannah Arendt, *On Revolution,* Viking, New York, 1965.
5. Karl Marx and Frederich Engels, *The Communist Manifesto,* International Publishers; and Frederich Engels, *Socialism: Utopian and Scientific,* International Publishers.
6. Juliet Mitchell, *Women's Estate,* Pantheon, New York, 1971.

Chapter Two

The Marxist
Concept of Revolution

The Marxist concept of revolution is that the means of production should be taken away from those who currently own them. But even after removal of productive properties from the once-ruling classes, women's oppression has continued in socialist countries. Socialists explain this, inadequately, in two ways: either as a problem of inherited consciousness and ideology lagging behind structural economic change; or as a problem of underdevelopment, forcing women to continue sacrificing equality no matter what class takes control. I have been pursuing a further problem: what other structural economic changes must be made to free women from oppression? Like a Marxist, I am looking for a material basis; but, like a feminist, I am looking for what is going on underneath the problems identified by Marxism as well.

Socialist strategic concepts on women have traditionally been based on Frederick Engels. However, his classic book was largely an historical reinterpretation of the precapitalist past. In *Origins of the Family, Private Property and the State*, he argued that the oppression of women arose with the rise of private property.[1] Only then did fathers need to control wives as heir-producers. Seizing the means of production, he aptly predicted, would also end the necessity of bequeathing private property to personal offspring.

Although such a long look backward might be helpful to understand how we got here today, it doesn't steer us very specifically toward the future, which is where a strategic argument should aim. Taking productive resources out of the wills of those who used to own them has not sufficiently changed the position of women. On the one hand, perhaps negating the origin of the oppression might not automatically cancel out the nature of the oppression in its current historical form. On the other hand, perhaps underneath this bequeathing process lurks the fundamental structure remaining to be understood: *the sharing of survival resources across sex and age groups, via marriage and the family, among kin.* Natural or biological, social categories of analysis are necessary to understand the problems this creates for women under capitalism, if the problems of capitalism are to be overcome.

To make a system not-capitalist, it must first be understood what is capitalist. Such a theme of negation runs through the history of socialist economic theory, although such history is itself contorted by contending conceptions of planning. All concepts brought to bear in the course of planning a socialist economic system have been directly based on the understanding of the inherited problems. Most generally, since the economic problem of capitalism has been identified as the inequitable accumulation of productive resources in private hands, socialists attempt to cancel what came before, by socializing ownership of those resources in the state or in smaller collectivized entities. But many priority decisions must be made, even to move within these broadest outlines.

As an illustration, the 1920's in Russia is a most interesting period.[2] At that time, Bukharin, a leading economist, understood socialism's distinguishing characteristic to be its potential to overcome periodic disequilibrium.[3] Under capitalism, anarchic conditions created by competition meant that equilibrium was achieved only through periodic crises. Under socialism then, these destructive phases could be avoided by the deliberate establishment of new patterns of sectoral interdependence. It followed from this conception that, in trying to construct socialism, planners should hold the principle of proportionality to be the ultimate aim. Bukharin argued for policy recommendations such as planning investment in industry according to the amount of output which agriculture could buy. He thought that the goal of planning should be equilibrium in the economy achieved through balanced growth; and that this might come at the expense of the socialized sector by prolonging relations of dependence on international capitalism, with essentials purchased abroad and domestic production concentrated on consumer goods for which there would be a ready market.[4] Other economists proposed plans based on a different assumption: that the distinguishing characteristic of socialism was not its ability to plan balanced growth (achieved by planning production according to existing market conditions), but its ability to achieve social ownership of the centralized, most important means of production.[5] To these economists, construction of socialism meant the intense growth of a large scale, public heavy-industrial sector, even if disproportionalities ensued. These policy recommendations won out in history and materialized as the First Five Year Plan. These disagreements about what distinguishes socialism from capitalism, about what should be cancelled and counteracted, run through socialist economic theory, and (at least on the level of rationality) account for differences between various socialist camps. If capitalism's extreme tendency toward centralization which creates satellites of dependencies is seen as the most important economic problem, socialists plan for self-reliance among cooperative units. If an economic problem is seen in capitalistic disproportionality between agricultural and industrial production and provision of services, socialists plan to reverse the proportion of investment devoted to each kind of economic activity. To wit, socialist planning concepts comprise a series of negations of the status quo. The Soviet Union still sees itself as socialist, though its economy runs on a system of profits, because profits are put to use for a different, non-capitalist purpose: the profits might take a capitalist form, but they serve a socialist function, that of negating the past or cancelling out crucial components of the previous order.[6]

The lesson being: that which is identified as crucial in the operation of capitalism becomes determinant in formation of priorities and planning method. *Yet Marxist class analysis abstracts away from differences based on sex and age,* as if incidental to the economic order; and socialists have no plan to overcome the resulting problems. Consequently, I am proposing kin categories, arising from sex and age differences, within classes. Through an analysis of the different positions of sex and age groupings within the class structure, in relation to economic power, the inadequacies of the traditional Marxist conception of revolution are brought to light. After identifying the patriarchal component of Marx's thought system, as reflected in *Capital,* the groundwork for this proposition will be made evident. There we will see the "hole" that fostered a socialist economic theory (and, of course, practice) diverging so far from concrete planning to liberate women— although plans have been developed to accomplish other stated goals which can be foreseen within the future, such as industrialization within five years.

But I warn the reader that like the history of the theoretical problem itself this text will make a digression. For I am only human, and I am still controlled by my subject. After a re-reading of the basic Marxism of *Capital,* I will share the turning points in the conceptual evolution of socialist thinking on "the woman question." Comparing this point by point to feminist thinking on socialism or the results of socialist practice, I will show how the interaction of socialism and feminism leads in the direction of kin categorization for social analysis of class behavior as well. The fact of the matter is that I took the latter route of the investigation myself; but as a writer having sympathy with my readers, I will short-cut the suspense by sharing the results of the process first. Of course, there is more than kindness in this organizational decision. My research into the historical results of socialist practice, and my tracing of its evident shortcomings for feminism back to the original blindspots in Marx's overall schema, is an artificial process if considered as an exercise in itself. I want to explain how my own thinking grows out of the larger context of socialist and feminist interaction. For that contemporary theoretical environment is just as important, as it frames my approach.

Footnotes

1. Frederich Engels, *The Origin of the Family, Private Property, and the State,* International Publishers, New York.
2. E.H. Carr, *Socialism in One Country,* Penguin, Baltimore, p. 528, discusses the 1920's in Russia as the "struggle for the plan."
3. Nicholas Bukharin, "Notes of an Economist at the Beginning of a New Economic Year," in Nicholas Spulbar, *Foundations of Strategy for Economic Growth,* Indiana University Press, Bloomington, 1965.
4. E.H. Carr and R.W. Davies, *Foundations of a Planned Economy,* Vol. 1, Part II, Macmillan, New York, 1969, p. 288-289.
5. Stephen Cohen, *Bukharin and the Bolshevik Revolution,* Vintage, New York, 1975, e.g. Strumilin's "Answer to Our Critics;" Naum Jasny, *Soviet Economists of the 20's,* Cambridge University Press, 1972.
6. E.G. Lieberman, *Economic Methods and the Effectiveness of Production,* International Arts and Sciences Press, White Plains, 1971.

Chapter Three

Contemporary Marxist/ Feminist Interaction

I mentioned the socialist tradition of basing strategic concepts about women on Engels. Now, what do I mean by *tradition?* The dictionary explains how a tradition comes from the handing down orally of stories, beliefs, customs from generation to generation. A tradition is a long-established custom or practice that has the effect of unwritten law. In theology, among Jews, tradition refers to the unwritten religious code and doctrines handed down by Moses; among Christians, to the unwritten teachings regarded as handed down from Jesus to the Apostles; among the Moslems, to the sayings and acts attributed to Mohammed, not in the Koran, but orally transmitted.

Capital is the written text of Marxism. That book, in its three or four volumes, is diligently studied the way Moslems study the Koran, Jews read the Torah, and so on. Engels' application of Marxism to women, on the other hand, traditionally has been orally handed down. After all, the provocation of his exploration was in the political arena where people interact with each other directly. Only peripherally are their actions based on what they have read in books. In conversations, we see and hear and feel the politics of a position, and only incidentally refer to what has already been written down.

As a woman, my first interaction with Marxism, both as a system of beliefs and a practical method of analysis, was through dialogue; this led me to trace the memorable book down. This was due to the particular circumstances of my political awakening. In 1972 I was in Chile as a journalist photographing and writing about women; and in this context I "discovered" socialism. I was young enough to return to the U.S. and go back to college, and I already knew more or less what I wanted to read. I had all those Marxist books in my suitcase, handed to me by people active during the left-wing government of Allende. When I got back to the States, I found many teachers on campus who had been radicalized in political movements as graduate students before I arrived. As teachers but also as comrades in revolt, they allowed me to pursue these books as part of a legitimized "independent" course of study. In addition they lengthened my listings with many more references and bibliographies; attendence of their classes had a further broadening effect. I am well aware that this was an unusual and well-timed opportunity. For me there was also the factor that I didn't have to pay for school, so I could afford to be employed by a radical academic organization. Because this made politics the center of my life at the time, rather than politics after hours as is so often the case, I had time to read and pursue certain problems. But the tendency of many radical women is to read only political works about women. It is natural to select by topic, so don't mistake this as a put-down. Quite the contrary. There is the additional feminist realization that nothing could be read which would explain about women. In fact, most of what is written simply leaves out women or presents a shallow or male-biased view. Thus, out of necessity the women's movement has created its own generic form of study comparable to the study groups on the left where the classics of Marxism are read. By this I mean the consciousness-raising group where the experiences of each participating woman are shared, against the background of what has been read and written. In this context, feminist analysis has been generated more often through verbal tradition, in the here and now.

Pushed by the emergence of this form of feminism, in the late 1960's Margaret Benston was among the first to pick up where Engels left off nearly a hundred years before. Her 1969 *Monthly Review* article, "The Political Economy of Women's Liberation," helped to establish Engels as the Marxist starting point for contributions to feminism. Then, in 1972 Eleanor Leacock wrote an introduction to an International Publishers' reprint of Engel's book. Together, these initial efforts concentrated energies around two points.

Many feminists were attracted to the field of anthropology to support or criticize Engels' analysis of the origins of women's oppression. This precipitated the matriarchy debate concerning women's status in pre-class systems. Engels had argued that only with the rise of private property did fathers need wives under their control, as producers of offspring who would become their heirs; the question was whether there was such a thing as a matriarchy before the rise of private property and the state. Was the position of women that much better? Some feminists argued that the problem was deeper and longer; that women have been universally oppressed, albeit in different forms, since the beginning of time. Though the matriarchy debate revolves around the past, Paula Webster, one of the early contributors, points out in "Matriarchy: A Vision of Power," "its real value lies in the future...in its rejection of power in the hands of men, regardless of the form of social organization, it pushes women (and men) to imagine a society that is not patriarchal."[1]

A second off-shoot from this return to Engels was along economic lines, more directly concerned with strategic questions. Following Benston, many began to apply concepts derived from Marx in the study of capitalist production to the "question" of women. This trend came partly from the unequal development of theory on women when compared to the amount of theory on capitalism. This comparative disadvantage led many to cling tightly to any theoretical constructs that were available, to clumsily glue together the little we knew about women in a Marxist framework. Picking up where Engels "stopped" has only served to exacerbate this process. His strategic position was based on a concept of "double duty," or double work load, which will be discussed more fully later on. Let a summary suffice here to indicate the problem as he saw it: while the proletarian wife enters production, her domestic duties remain a noose around her neck; but this last economic function of the household—service production for family members—would soon follow goods production out of the private home into publicly organized industry as well. Benston wrote in 1969 that this work of the wife in the home produced *use values,* meaning that the work was necessary and useful but that it did not create wealth for the capitalists. Others, primarily Mariarosa Dalla Costa in her pamphlet from Italy, *The Power of Women and the Subversion of the Community* argued that housework produced *surplus value,* meaning that the wife added to the wealth of the capitalist by work performed for her husband in the home by keeping down the necessary level of wages.[2]

This updated version of Engels' argument about the housewife's double duty made a dual contribution. First some points were established—that housework could not just gradually remove itself from the home; that just as workers battle to make gains in factories, special struggle would be required to move that socialization process along. To bring about such a socialization of housework, some began to argue that wages be paid to the housewife. In arguing for tactical employment of "wages for housework" as an organizing demand, Dalla Costa and others made unconventional use of the traditional Marxist notion of surplus value. Those who took issue with their conclusion developed a facility to carry out Marxist method of analysis. Therefore, the debate helped clarify the limitations of the inherited Marxist concepts. Secondly, the debate provided an exercise to practice Marxist thinking and new notions appropriate to the material at hand were percolated in the process. For example, in "Loom, Broom and Womb," which appeared in *Frontiers*, the Women's Work Study Group coined the term *household mode of production*.[3] In the household, they went on to explain, a variety of economic functions are performed, which will not just gradually wither away even as some service production is relocated outside the home. In *Radical America* Renate Bridenthal talked about "The Dialectics of Production and Reproduction in History" in the new sense of a *mode of reproduction*.[4] Among other things, she used this term to explain that relocating service production—or the work of reproducing laborers—outside of the home created a special labor market for women, almost tangential to the mode of goods production "proper." Amy Bridges and I, starting out by working on a critique of Dalla Costa, finished off with a concept of consumption work. In a *Monthly Review* article, "The Other Side of the Paycheck," we discussed the new activities created for the housewife by the proliferation of the service sector which required her to interact with a range of people outside the home: in supermarkets, schools, clinics, etc.[5] These concepts were particularly helpful in grappling with the dynamics of change, rather than statically describing what goes on repeatedly within the four walls of the home. In addition, they highlight *processes* rather than social structures by asking the questions: what activities are being moved from where to where? These ideas are valuable in overcoming the segmented analysis of women's role within the family versus women's role within the workplace, as originally dichotomized by Engels' notion of the "double duty."

Meanwhile, radical feminism had already shot off in another direction because of the inability of the traditionally dichotomized Marxian economic approach to answer the questions that feminism raised. Simone de Beauvoir's *Second Sex* was perhaps the initiator of this trend. Published in the U.S. in 1952, it was influential in the rebirth of American feminist thinking a decade later. De Beauvoir concluded her chapter "The View of Historical Materialism" by rejecting what she called the "economic monism of Engels." She wrote that other levels of existence must be understood beyond technology, since "in Engels' account of the history of the family the most important developments seem to arise according to the caprices of mysterious fortune." In 1970 Shulamith Firestone picked this up in *The Dialectic of Sex* to support the argument that beneath the economic system lay the psychosexual roots motivating class, and that these roots demanded analysis to comprehend the problems of women.[6] Basically, she accepted Marxian analysis of the economy as far as it went; but she argued that since the Marxian notion of *socialist revolution* had been derived on the basis of economic analysis only, a further concept of *feminist revolution* would be required to direct the struggle for social change on behalf of women. Kate Millet's analysis of the Soviet Union in *Sexual Politics* made clear that even with a socialist revolution an antifeminist counter-revolution might set in.[7] So radical feminism began with the conclusion that a revolution to change the economic system was necessary, but not sufficient, to liberate women.

Socialist-feminism then emerged. This became the vein of socialists who adopted the last part of radical feminist analysis—that the liberation of women demanded more than a change in the economic system. Socialist-feminists and radical feminists disagree about whether sex or class is "primary;" i.e.,which form of oppression is a symptom and which is the original problem, again bringing up the matriarchy debates over the situation of women in pre-class society. But there is a forward-looking strategic area in which the two groups at least in part agree: that the "other than economic" concerns of the radical feminists require special consideration. Such insistence distinguishes socialist-feminists from other socialists, who still believe that the basic economic change proposed by Marx will allow for the gradual evolution of equal status for women. This is important for modern feminists to understand, due to the weight that this philosophy holds in current socialist systems.

An example of the kind of socialist thinking that would resist the common ground shared by radical feminists and socialist-feminists appeared in the "Women and the Economy" issue of the *Review of Radical Political Economics*. Harold Barnett, in "The Political Economy of Rape and Prostitution," wrote, "if *sexism is primary*—as is argued by Kate Millet, Shulamith Firestone, and the New York Radical Feminists—then the observed patterns of enforcement and victimization vis-a-vis rape and prostitution represent the manifestation of sexism in capitalist society. If capitalism is replaced by socialism we should expect that *a different pattern* of rape and prostitution will be observed. If *private ownership of property is the primary contradiction,* argued in varying forms by Frederich Engels, Juliet Mitchell...then rape and prostitution are manifestations of the need of capitalism to oppress women. We should thus expect to find a *significant decline and eventual elimination* of rape and prostitution in socialist countries."[8] Thus Barnett makes Juliet Mitchell and other contemporary socialist-feminists sound stupid. If they thought rape and prostitution and other forms of oppression of women would automatically self-destruct after abolishment of private property, why would they be interested in feminism at all? And I add the emphasis to draw out the implication: if two kinds of feminists disagree about origins, their strategic orientations must diverge.

Although in some senses we know this to be true from politics, I repeat for emphasis: socialist-feminists have taken from radical feminists the notion that the economic change of socializing the means of production is not a sufficient strategy to provoke an "eventual elimination" of problems concerning women. For example, Juliet Mitchell concludes *Psychoanalysis and Feminism* by calling for "a specific struggle against patriarchy" and by suggesting that "women with revolutionary feminism can be the spearhead of general ideological change as the working class is the agent of the overthrow of the specifically capitalist mode of production."[9] This does not ring so different from Firestone's original suggestion a few years earlier that women's role is to analyze and make the sex revolution, because Marxist analysis and the left are making the labor revolution.

But it has proven all too easy to foreclose the

notion of *feminist revolution* in the socialist-feminist view. In the introduction to her 1972 *Women, Resistance and Revolution,* for example, Sheila Rowbotham made just such a foreclosure, writing that her book was part of a "continuing effort to connect *feminism* to *socialist revolution.*"[10] The idea of feminist revolution drops out of view. Why not, for example, "connect socialism to feminist revolution?" The felt-emphasis is very different. Redstockings, a survivor-group of the New York Radical Feminists, criticized the socialist-feminists for artificially or prematurely forging these connections, or "uniting everything with hyphens," as they wrote in their 1975 publication *Feminist Revolution.*[11] This they point out, dilutes the specifically feminist strategies, goals and concepts. Amy Bridges and Heidi Hartmann have traced just such a process in socialist-feminist writings and dubbed it "The Unhappy Marriage of Marxism and Feminism."[12] There they call for a "more progressive union," taking progress to mean movement forward rather than regression back to where we were before the notion of feminist revolution came to the fore.

Unfortunately, the concept of feminist revolution doesn't seem to have been articulated well enough to check this process of absorption. About the most succinct statement of it was made by Ti-Grace Atkinson in *Amazon Odyssey,*[13] where she said that while workers must take control of the capitalists' means of production, women must take control of our own productive properties—our wombs. Thus woman's control of woman's body constitutes the material, physical basis of a feminist revolution;

and many single issues are tactics with that strategic view in mind: abortion reform, rape resistance, the fight against domestic violence, the protestation against alienation from our bodies by the medical system. From this point of view, the fight against mediating structures which remove this control further from our own hands is also part of the revolution: changing divorce laws, passing legislation pertaining to equal rights in work.

From this perspective of feminist revolution, a wife is owned in marriage as a piece of productive property, analogous to the machine in the capitalist factory. On the other hand, Marxist analysis has viewed the wife as analogous to the laborer, which has set another dichotomization into Marxist thinking on women. Previously, the double duty concept referred to *work on the job* plus *work in the family;* now the double duty concept still refers to work *on the job,* but increasingly to *ideology* in the family. Within this schema many of the breakthroughs in feminist theory have been neatly stuck back on top of existing Marxist analysis without comprehension of their truly *revolutionary* feminist character. In *Capitalism, the Family, and Personal Life,* for example, Eli Zaretsky argues that Engels was correct in his analysis of the gradual disintegration of the economic functions of the family as the locus of work changes and factories are built up outside the home; the trouble is, he asserts, the ideological functions linger in the domestic sphere; the production of beliefs, attitudes, emotional support systems.

Bridges and Hartmann have warned against the tendency to collapse feminist concerns back into what is understood as the ideological structure of capitalism. Patriarchy has concrete material existence which must be systematically analyzed too, and then we must see how these discrete systems interact. Gayle Rubin, an anthropologist, has moved the debate to one more level of abstraction, which unwittingly has the side effect of reinforcing the dichotomization. She has argued (in a paper which will be discussed more fully)[14] that we need separate analysis of the *sex gender system*, as the organization of gender might not always be patriarchal; then we should see how this interacts with the mode of production, which likewise might not always be capitalistic. Furthering the thinking of Firestone, Rubin wants to initiate a political economy of sex, analogous to Marx's political economy of labor in the production of commodities. I agree that we need a political economy of sex, but unfortunately this dichotomization continues to encourage the mistaken assumption that Marx's original critique of political economy was acceptable. When perhaps, since his critique was sex blind, as Rubin has noted, his analysis of production was a bit "off base" too. Thus, isn't it possible that we might find his concept of how to revolutionize production inadequate, and not merely the series of Marxist suggestions for liberating women? I would rather pose the question what is the *sexual political economy of production* than what is the *political economy of sex*.

Approached from either end, the problem remains: what can we contribute to the analysis of the nature of feminist revolution? Mitchell has suggested revolutionizing the unconscious. Since the unconscious develops its tenacity in the family, Rubin has suggested a revolution in the kinship structure. Since a specific kinship structure upholds a specific economic system of production, we could still make advances on these first two questions by asking: what further economic changes would be needed, besides taking control of the means of production? To explore this, we need to re-examine the original economic analysis of Marx, not only specifically about women, but about class and the organization of material production. From this we might gain an awareness of the initial patriarchal bias of Marx's entire framework. Then, in the interaction of women's liberation and socialism—as theories and as social movements—we can see reflected the interaction of patriarchy and capitalism, the intertwining of sex gender and the economic production system. My case study of theoretical-political intersection must be seen as part of this larger endeavor, for the concepts which I will examine didn't arise "all by themselves," nor did the political movements in which they were spawned. However, I feel that dissecting the notions which people express in action for change can reveal what is at heart wrong with the system. For people are only saying in a refined form what is really bothering them, ostensibly for greater communication.

Footnotes

1. Recently reprinted in *Toward an Anthropology of Women*, Rayna Reiter, ed. Monthly Review. New York, 1975.
2. Mariarosa Dalla Costa and Selma James, *The Power of Women and the Subversion of the Community*. Falling Wall Press. Bristol, England, 1972.
3. "Loom, Broom and Womb: Producers, Maintainers and Reproducers," Women's Work Study Group, originally appeared in *Frontiers*, Vol. I, No. 2; and has since been reprinted in *Radical America*, Vol. 10, No. 2, March-April 1976.
4. Renate Bridenthal, "The Dialectics of Production and Reproduction in History," in *Radical America*, Vol. 10, No. 2, March-April 1976.
5. Amy Bridges and Batya Weinbaum, "The Other Side of the Paycheck," *Monthly Review*, July-August 1976. This has recently been reprinted, along with several other important articles in these debates, in Zillah Eisenstein's *Capitalist Patriarchy: The Case for Socialist Feminism*. Monthly Review Press. New York, 1978.
6. Shulamith Firestone, *The Dialectic of Sex: The Case for Feminist Revolution*. Bantam. New York, 1970.
7. Kate Millet, *Sexual Politics*. Doubleday and Co. Garden City, New York, 1970.
8. Harold Barnett, "The Political Economy of Rape and Prostitution," in *Review of Radical Political Economics*, Vol. 8, No. 1, Spring, 1976, p. 64. Throughout the text, emphasis has been added by the author to stress certain quoted phrases.
9. Juliet Mitchell, *Psychoanalysis and Feminism*. Pantheon. New York, 1974, p. 414.
10. Sheila Rowbotham, *Women, Resistance and Revolution*. Pantheon. New York, 1972, p. 11.
11. *Feminist Revolution* is available from Red Stockings, P.O. Box 413, New Paltz, New York.
12. Amy Bridges and Heidi Hartmann, "The Unhappy Marriage of Marxism and Feminism," in *Women and Revolution*. Lydia Sargent, ed. South End Press. Boston, 1979.
13. Ti-Grace Atkinson, *Amazon Odyssey*. Links Books. New York, 1974.
14. In Reiter, *op. cit.*

Chapter Four

The Patriarchal
Component of Marxism

Division of labor by sex and age is one of the most basic mechanisms that keeps the economic system, as well as the kinship structure and a debilitating unconscious, bearing full weight upon us. The first division of labor (by sex) creates the material basis for women's oppression by forcing us into economic dependencies on men; the second division of labor (by age) creates the material basis for patriarchy by forcing economic dependency on fathers—both generic and biological. In this section, I will both demonstrate these omissions in Marxist theory and indicate what I see as some of the cumulative consequences.

In the beginning, Marx wrote, "there springs up naturally a division of labor caused by differences of sex and age..." This division, based on a purely physiological foundation, "enlarges its materials by the expansion of the community, by the increase of property relations, especially by the concept of free enterprise..."[1] As money arose at the point of exchange between families, tribes, and communities, the existing differences worsened. He noted that this process somehow benefited the collective production of the larger society. I would like to figure out how, but I cannot do so by using Marx's categories. For when Marx went on to analyze the economy, or the collective production of the larger society, he did so in class terms, abstracting away from differences based on sex and age:

> The value of labor power is determined by the necessaries of life habitually required by the *average* laborer. The quantity of these necessities is known in any given epoch of a given society, and can therefore be treated as a constant magnitude. What changes is the value of these quantities. There are, besides, two factors which enter into the determination in the value of labor power. One, *the expenses of developing that power,* which expenses vary with the mode of production; and, the other, its natural diversity, *the difference between the labor power of men and women, of children and adults.* The employment of these different sorts of labor power, an employment which is, in its turn, made necessary by the mode of production, makes a great difference in the cost of maintaining the family of the laborer, and in the value of the labor power of the adult male. *Both these factors, however, are excluded from the following investigation.*[2]

Herein lies the patriarchal component of Marx's method, so let's examine it more closely. First, consider the concept "average laborer," used interchangeably with "the adult male." When different wages are paid out to the laborers, according to sex and age, there cannot be an "average" laborer. If a capitalist employs three workers, he then pays, let's say, $5 an hour to the adult male, $3 to the women, and $1 to a 16 year-old boy. The average would be calculated by adding five plus three plus one and then dividing the total by three, equalling 9/3, or $3 an hour. But so what? This average rate doesn't bring the boy any more, and still leaves the woman unequal vis-a-vis the man. Concrete reality does not uphold the abstraction of an average laborer, an average value of labor power, or an average wage. The abstract concept obscures the on-going differentials; thus we cannot detect how these differences benefit the collective production in society or how the structure of collective production exacerbated those differences.

Family budgets illustrate the other side of the coin. Take a household surviving on $14,000 a year, in which the adult male laborer brings in $10,000 and his wife, $4,000. Does this mean the average income per family member is $7,000 a year? What good does this do one of our so-called "average members" when she wants to get a divorce? She still has to live on $4,000 alone, given the *real* fall-offs in child support and alimony payments. Aggregates, medians, and averages always skew the reality this way, as you might recall by thinking of how the corporations use the "average" trick when talking about the Third World. Ralston-Purina, for example, defends its agribusiness investments in Columbia by saying "the average nutrient intake has risen since our poultry farm expansions..." This neglects how the nutrient intake has risen in the upper class and fallen in the lower, since the latter can't afford Ralston-Purina fryers on the market.[3]

Next, let's pick up on the matter of leaving out the expenses of developing labor power. This is the unpaid work of the "adult female," not the paid work of the "adult male." Later in the same volume, Marx explains that he leaves this out because it has been the convenience of the capitalist to do so:

> The laborer consumes in a two-fold way. While producing he consumes by his labor the means of production, and converts them into products with higher value than that of the capitalist who bought it. On the other hand, the laborer turns the money paid to him for his labor power, into means of subsistence: this is his *individual consumption*. The laborer's productive consumption, and his individual consumption, are therefore totally distinct. In the former, he acts as the motive power of capital and belongs to the capitalist. In the latter, *he belongs to himself, and performs his necessary vital function outside the process of production...*[4]

At this juncture, his "average laborer" has become "the individual." Marx is still discussing not the whole class but the adult male in the class removed from the real context of survival activities necessary for consumption. In this omission the significance of abstracting away from differences based on sex and age within the class becomes apparent. The economic basis for cross-sex-and-age groups formed by working class individuals for survival (e.g., households) has not been analyzed. These two "oversights" misconstruct the position of women within the class; and further, a basic economic dynamic within the class; and therefore, between the class and the directors of collective production.

In this light, consider the previous quote in its larger context:

> When treating the working day, we saw that the laborer is often compelled to make his individual consumption a mere incident of production. In such a case, *he supplies himself with the necessaries in order to maintain his labor power,* just as coal and water are supplies to the steam engine and oil to the wheel. His means of consumption, in that case, are the mere means of consumption required by a means of production; his individual consumption is directly productive consumption. This, however, appears to be an abuse not essentially pertaining to capitalist production.
> The matter takes quite another aspect, when we contemplate, not the single capitalist, and the *single laborer,* but the capitalist class and the laboring class, not an isolated process of production, but capitalist production in full swing, and on its actual social scale.[5]

Think of the laborers you might know; or better yet, think of your own working day. Thus you might remind yourself that "the laborer" does not supply himself with necessaries in order to maintain his own labor power. More often "he" gets a wife to do so for him. Hence the structural difficulty of surviving either as an unmarried or woman worker. (The combination is horrendous.) Wouldn't something be gained by moving from "the single laborer" category to a categoric relation to the household, before abstracting to the dimension of "the laboring class?" For individuals do not *live* in classes, although they *work* in them; they live in households.

Although common sense tells us that workers do not float around out in space after working the day for the capitalist on the job, Marx continues to think in terms of the *"individual* consumption of the working *class."* He does so because he says "the capitalist may safely leave its fulfillment to the laborer's instinct of self-preservation and propagation."[6] Back to biology again. But if Marx had taken such a step as I am recommending, and then gone on to the level of abstraction reached in the "laboring class," his analysis of class relations—both economic and political—necessarily would have come down to us in a considerably altered form; household relations modify production relations, as well as the other way around.

Let me share a narrative of working class life written by a New York City settlement worker in 1924, as common material in which to locate some of the left-gray area. Rheta Childe Dorr, in her autobiography, is discussing here the friends she made with Lower East Side "girl wage-earners."

Living thus among the mass of the workers, where every single member of the family, except the mother, was a wage earner from his 14th birthday, I saw how far from accidental was the presence of women in the working world. *Even a superficial survey of family budgets revealed that without money contributions from all the children, girls included, no working-class family in the modern world could exist.* A little thought, a little reading revealed that without the productive labor of women the working class family never did exist. The only difference between the old-time families and the new was that *women were once unpaid industrial drudges and now they carried home pay-envelopes to be added to the family income. How had economists, employees, trade-unionists come to overlook such a simple fact as that?* The historians of the eighteenth century industrial revolution recorded that in pre-factory days each weaver of cloth had to have five spinners working all the time to supply him with yarn. The spinners-wives, daughters, unmarried sisters were paid no money, but that did not alter their status as producers and creators of wealth.

The East Side of New York City where I lived had been German before it was Jewish and great sections of the quarter were given over to the tailoring trade, then a home industry. *The average household consisted of a father, a skilled tailor, one or two journeymen, and a number of female 'dependents.'* All these 'dependents' worked in the tailoring trade, but *no one recognized them.* I remember meeting in Brooklyn an aged German woman who had formerly lived in my neighborhood, and she gave me a graphic account of her connection with the tailoring trade. Her job was running seams on the clumsy sewing machines of her day, and afterwards she worked a few more hours helping her mother cook, clean, wash and iron. *Sometimes her father rented out her services to other tailors, of course taking her wages.* When at 19 *she married a journeyman in her father's employ,* she had the audacity to claim as a right a few dollars with which to buy her wedding finery. 'Mine father he licked me good' she cackled as she related this piece of youthful wildness. Her husband, for whom she worked 25 years, would probably have 'licked her good' had she ever suggested drawing a bit of a wage, and so might *her son* for whom she stitched until his inherited tailor shop was absorbed into the big factory.[7]

She described how even among the factory workers of the East Side "no girl regarded her earnings as her own. All handed in their pay-envelopes unopened and the pittance they received they looked on as a gift from their fathers." She wrote that "a shrewd father demanded from the bridegroom a money compensation for the loss of his daughter's wages." [8]

From this slice of history we can learn the following lesson. Individuals once pooled *labor* in families. Yet once capitalists have collectivized production outside the home, the dislocated family members now pool *wages*. This economic basis coheres the household unit, even though production has largely been socialized outside the domestic realm. Households of laborers, and thus laborers, survive on money contributed by many sex and age groups. Thus the concept of the single, individual laborer, dispossessed of everything but "his" labor power to sell to the capitalist, is erroneous. As our twentieth century tailors on the Lower East Side lost their shops (their means of production, their productive property), they also lost their daughters' labor; but they continued to claim the benefits of that labor, via the wage.

Marx freed himself from analyzing economic relations such as these. It is this component of his thought which I ask you to reflect upon as patriarchal; that is, the posing of the point of view of the "old man"—the father, the patriarch, the adult male—as if this singular vantage point represented the point of view of all class members. In the beginning, if you remember, Marx acknowledged differences based on sex and age, which worsened at the point of exchange between families with the rise of the free enterprise system; yet he proceeded to calculate the value of labor power on the basis of an average. In doing so, he abstracted away from (1) the acknowledged differences based on sex and age; and (2) the real circumstances of the laborer's subsistence activities. Thus freed, Marx focuses on a discussion of the point of view and problems of the adult male laborer as he competes with the capitalist for the role of protagonist in the Marxist novel. As a feminist, I must protest the claim to objectivity when the position of the father within the working class is "scientifically" designated to be synonymous with the point of view of all sex and age groups in the class. Similarly, Marxists protest the bourgeois ideologist's claim to "objectivity" when social science is portrayed as if free of specific class interests.

And since we have come this far in cutting the jugular vein of Marx's patriarchal position, let's go another step to recognize the tradition of locating the struggle of the class in the *struggle between two subsets within the larger social category of father.* Return to our Lower East Side tailor for illustration. Working class fathers lost their shops and their daughter's labor to other fathers who had accumulated more. Although Marx noted that the capitalist mode of exploitation swept away the economic base of parental authority,[9] he might have been more specific in light of these real developments in the working class: *one group of fathers transformed the economic power of another group of fathers.* Marx noted that with the introduction of machinery there was a deviation from his adult-male-head-of-the-household norm. At this historical juncture he identified the interference of other antagonists of the father—his wife and offspring—with what he analyzed as a relation primarily between two groups (or classes) of adult men:

...The value of the *adult laborer* was determined, not only by the labor-time necessary to maintain the *individual* adult laborer, but also by that to maintain *his family*. Machinery, by throwing every member of that family on to the labor market, spreads the value of *the man's labor* power over his whole family. It thus depreciates *his* labor power.[10]

To Marx this represents a problem to be resolved categorically through "the head of the family" or the adult male. The question for analysis is his rate of exploitation. Thus, while Marx talked about other sex and age groups, his way of doing so was patriarchal.

Marx did go on to posit that by going into production other sex and age groups would become like other "individual workers" (i.e., like adult males) in their relation to the capitalist.[11] Marx based his faith for this equalizing potential on what he mistakenly thought of as the "obvious fact" of the "collective working group being composed of individuals of both sexes and all ages."[12] Having built his categories of analysis on an abstraction away from differences based on sex and age, he curiously bases the *solution* of those differences on his own *assumptions* of the working unity in production among the differently sexed and aged individuals. He had argued that sex and age differences are biological, that they give rise to a "natural" division of labor, and that the production structure built up outside the household exacerbates this "natural" state. How, then, can the (unanalyzed) *intensification* of the differences overcome them?

In fact, those differences are not natural. An-thropologist Gayle Rubin has drawn from Levi-Strauss to reformulate the argument:

> Although every society has some sort of division of tasks by sex, the assignment of any particular task to one sex or the other varies enormously. In some groups, agricul-ture is the work of women, in others, the work of men. Women carry the heavy bur-dens in some societies, men in others. There are even examples of female hunters and warriors, and of men performing child care tasks. Levi-Strauss concludes from a survey of the division of labor by sex that it is not a biological specialization, but must have some other purpose. This purpose, he argues, is to insure the union of men and women by making the smallest viable economic unit contain at least one man and one woman.[13]

Thus the household, which Marx "assumed away," along with the sex and age division of labor, might deter equal participation in production (as I will show Engels argued). But the reverse is true as well: unequal participation in production might reinforce the household. Sex and age division of labor in the collective structure of production might continually require the pooling of resources across sex and age lines, among kin tied together via family relations. At least a dialectical dynamic operates between these two unanalyzed realms; therefore "women into production" cannot be the unifying solution that Marxism hopefully asserts it to be. Let us return to our example of the tailor's daughters.

Might not the "girl wage earner" be forced into a subservient relation to her father by her capitalist employer's reluctance to give her a sole-supporting wage? Or by her father's organization of trade unions to protect the disenfranchised rights of the adult male worker, at the same time seizing for himself a hierarchical position over others, both on the job and in the home?[14]

Footnotes

1. Karl Marx, *Capital,* Vol.I, p. 351, International Publishers, New York, 1970.
2. *Ibid.,* p. 519.
3. For the use of this argument, see *Food First!* by Joe Collins and Frances Lappe, Houghton Mifflin Co., Boston, 1977.
4. Marx, *op.cit.,* p. 571-3.
5. *Loc. cit.*
6. *Loc. cit.*
7. Rheta Childe Dorr, *A Woman of Fifty,* Funk and Wagnalls, New York, 1924.
8. *Ibid., p.*
9. Marx, *op.cit.,* p. 490.
10. *Ibid.,* p. 395.
11. *Ibid.,* p. 489.
12. *Ibid.,* p. 490.
13. Gayle Rubin, "The Traffic in Women: Notes on the 'Political Economy' of Sex," in Rayna Reiter's *Toward an Anthropology of Women,* Monthly Review Press, New York, 1977, p.178.
14. A perusal of more recent material on the immigrant Jewish experience illustrates the under belly of the disenfranchised-

father coin, leading one to speculate how much the displacement of the economic father in the immigrant home might have been a motivating force in early Jewish radicalism which helped build trade unions and socialist organizations. As Irving Howe writes in his discussion of themes in Jewish-socialist literature, "in the turmoil of the American city, traditional family patterns could not survive. The dispossession and shame of many immigrant fathers has been a major subject for fiction about immigrant Jews, both in English and Yiddish. For the Jewish wife the transition seems to have been a little easier. Having sold herring in the market place of her *shtetl*, she could sell herrings on Orchard Street—and then, if a little more ambitious, open a grocery or dry goods store. Never having regarded herself as part of a spiritual elite, she did not suffer so wrenching a drop in status and self-regard as her husband. She was a practical person, she had mouths to feed, and by and large, she saw to it that they were fed." (*World of Our Fathers,* Harcourt Brace, New York, 1976, p.173.) This part was also played by daughters, such as the main character of Anzia Yezierska's *Breadgivers* who took to the streets to sell herrings as a young girl. The psychological effects on the economically-undermined fathers must have been severe; consequently, as Howe further notes about the wife in a novel of the same period: in spite of economic dislocations, she was "able to maintain the traditional, patriarchal structure. Pauline, a sensitive woman, declared that the children should not give their household contributions to her, even though she did the shopping and spent most of the cash. She understood the humiliation of Isaac (the unemployed father) and worked to preserve his old role and status, declaring that 'papa should be the manager, he being the head of the household.' Thus the forms, if not the substance of family relations were maintained at the Jacobson home."

Chapter Five

Marxism is a Strategy for Change

Many nineteenth century thinkers, philosophers and political theorists (particularly those whose books form the basis of university disciplines today) generalized a world view from the position of the father; and they too obscured the patriarchal interactions. In *Love's Body*, Norman O. Brown (a neo-Freudian populist), in positing that all conventional Anglo-Saxon political theory is patriarchal, discussed Durkheim's concept of division of labor:

> Durkheim in his book on the division of labor saw two distinct principles, antagonistic and complementary, as warp and woof of social organization, which he called mechanical and organic solidarity. *Mechanical solidarity is union based on likeness; and it finds its clearest expression in kinship.* Organic solidarity is union based on

differentiation and organic interdependence; its expression is the division of labor. Durkheim associates mechanical solidarity not only with the family but also with the collective conscience and with criminal law as a repressive system—in Freudian terms the super-ego and the father.[1]

Marx was just as fixed within a patriarchal tradition as Durkheim, even though Marx did break with the bourgeois tradition. That is, while he noted sex and age differences, he continued to use categories that treated all kin as indistinguishable.

But the difference between Marx and Durkheim and other conventional theorists is that Marxism is a doctrine for social change and social action. From Marxist analysis we are given to understand that to change their unequal situation women must first get into production; and once there, participate as individuals in the collective struggle against the class oppressor. The point of dwelling on Marx's patriarchal bias is to give us a clearer conceptual understanding of the insufficiencies of his strategy for changing the social position of women. Engels' book, written in 1884, considerably after Marx's original treatise (Volume I appeared in 1867), necessarily took up some of the areas Marx had selected to avoid. I say necessarily because the socialist movement had to, since an international feminist movement was developing its own strategic conceptions at the time. "During the last third of the nineteenth century," writes Edith Hurwitz, in an article entitled "The International Sisterhood," "hundreds and even thousands of women from all European nations were turning their backs on the male-dominated politics of their homelands and forming their own international."[2] Thus, "woman" became a question in nineteenth century Marxism in much the same way that rape, prostitution, and physical abuse of women became a question in twentieth century Marxism— after the independent feminist movement had raised it loudly.

Let us not forget that the nineteenth century women's movement was perhaps the most powerful influence upon the character of the western world of that era. This has been argued by Theodore Roszak, and stressed by Sheila Collins as a factor motivating the emergence of patriarchal theories in this period.[3] I stress the scope of the early wave of feminism when discussing Engels, because a recent tendency has been to suppose we bring a newly-feminist eye to Marxism. This error partly stems from tracing the history of women as a "question" *within* Marxism without looking at the Feminism which Marxism, in arguing that the strategy for class revolution was necessarily the strategy for women, has had to interact with historically. I am not going to redress that grievance here, for I am not an historian. My aim is only to indicate the political context of Engels' theoretical contribution in *Origins*.

Marx had altered nineteenth century social theory by talking about the "individual" in the working class, instead of the abstract bourgeois "individual" in (presumably classless) "society." But nineteenth century feminism already had been talking for quite some time about the fact that the rights of the individual—bourgeois or other—did not include the rights of women. Hence Mary Wollstone-craft's 1792 *Vindications of the Rights of Woman* rapidly led to the enactment of the political conclusion that women should organize a special struggle to get the rights of other individuals in society.[4] And the strategy was to start with the basic right, the right to know, embodied in the right to vote. German women participated in this international suffrage movement also. By 1869 the first feminist organization had been founded in Germany.[5] Although the socialist international and the workingmen's organizations under their auspices were working on extended voting rights to all men, with or without property, they did not support the struggle for voting rights of women.[6] This they considered bourgeois: working class men, it was held, should get the vote first; they, in turn, could *choose* to vote in the right to vote for women. This was the context of *Origins*, in which Engels argued that the answer to the "woman question" was the overall change recommended by the socialists, the socializing of private property. The politically repressive laws of Bismarck in the 1880's added to the force of the argumentation by throwing both the socialist and the women's organizations underground. Although not purely tactical, Engels' argument did start with the political conclusion that women should fight with everyone else to seize the means of production. If one reads the argument forward, we are bequeathed the socialist strategy for liberating women in the future. As the argument is reasoned backwards, we have inherited a concept which explains the origins of our oppression in the past. What was obscured by the direction of the logic was any basis for change in the present.

Marx's notion of change was that it came about through struggle. If he foresaw change in the differential status of the sexes, he surely expected struggle to bring about that change. In this respect, the first wave of feminism was correct in what it tried to do, even when considered from a Marxist perspective. Struggle for the individual rights of women would hasten the time when differences based on sex and age would disappear. But the core of Engels' argument was: you don't need special struggle for rights now—you need revolution. With this, though revolutionary in its totality, Marxist theory presented a concept which was fundamentally evolutionary when it came to women. In the context of the socialist international's proposition that women leave off struggling directly for women's equality, Engels offered a conceptual rationale for taking part instead in the "one big struggle." By this he meant the working class fight for socialist revolution, which would, if successful, pave the way for the gradual evolution of equality for women. It was conceded that women's entrance into production had not yet given women all the rights of "individuals" under capitalism. But after private ownership of the means of production had been abolished, productivity would be socialized by the state. Investment capital would be available to remove all service functions from the realm of the private household. Engels argued that it was her domestic duties that prevented the proletarian wife from attaining equality in the public realm under capitalism. "If she carries out her duties," he wrote, "in the private service of her family, she remains excluded from social production and unable to earn; and if she wants to take part in public production and earn independently, she cannot carry out her family duties." "But," he went on, "with the transfer of the means of production into common ownership, the single family ceases to be the basic economic unit of society."[7] The state could pay to reorganize, publicly, her "family duties," chores of "household management," "private housekeeping," and "care and education of children." Thus, once freed to work in the socialized realm as a true individual, the equal rights of the proletarian *wife* would follow. Therefore, the fight for socialism would serve as a tool to end the economic basis of the family, ending the distorted relations between men and women.

Working backwards from the political priority of "one big struggle," Engels' conceptual argument ended up in the same place as far as strategic recommendation. Although "the first condition for the liberation of the wife is to bring the whole female sex back into public industry," this did not bring about equality under capitalism because of the double demands placed on the proletarian wife.[8] She had her private duties to perform for her husband and children at home as well as her tasks for the capitalist. Consequently, socialists participated in the struggle for protective legislation to limit what the wife could do on the job. Otherwise it was thought that her double duties might overwhelm her or discourage her from becoming a working member of the class at all. One wonders why the struggle was not to limit, instead, the chores she had to perform at home—but then one remembers how this was to be put off until private property had been overcome when the task could be accomplished by means of the socialized state. So it was still thought to be the problem of private property that oppressed the wife. After all, the family which now kept the wife busily servicing the family members in the privacy of her home first arose as a way for the father to bequeath private property to his heirs (her children). Thus the end of private property would end the economic basis of the family. As Engels wrote, "by transformation of by far the greater portion, at any rate, of permanent, heritable wealth—the means of production—into social property, the coming revolution will reduce to a minimum all this anxiety about bequeathing and inheriting."[9] So Engels concluded once again that relations between men and women could be better under socialism.

Footnotes

1. Norman O. Brown, *Love's Body,* Vintage, New York, 1966, p. 9.
2. In *Becoming Visible: Women in European History,* edited by Renate Bridenthal and Claudia Koonz, Houghton Mifflin, 1977.
3. Roszack, "The Hard and the Soft: The Force of Feminism in Modern Times," in *Masculine and Feminine,* Harper and Row, New York, 1969; Collins, *A Feminist Perspective of Religion:. A Different Heaven and a Different Earth,* Judson Press, Valley Forge, 1974.
4. Mary Wollstonecraft, *A Vindication of the Rights of Woman,* Norton. New York, 1972.
5. See Trevor Lloyd, *Suffragettes International,* New York, American Heritage Press, 1971, and Hugh Puckett, *Germany's Women Go Forward,* New York, Columbia University Press, 1930.
6. See Weiner Thönnessen, *The Emancipation of Women: The Rise and Decline of the Women's Movement in German Social Democracy, 1863-1933,* Pluto Press, London, 1973.
7. Frederich Engels, *The Origin of the Family, Private Property, and the State,* International Publishers. New York, 1972. p. 137.
8. *Ibid.,* pp. 137-138.
9. *Ibid.,* pp. 138-139.

Chapter Six

Socialism as a Take-Off
Point for Women's Liberation

Following Engels' circuitous argument, we have
two reasons to expect that socialism would liberate
women. The first is that under socialism the state
could use public resources to socialize private household "servicing;" second, the abolishment of private
property would end the father's anxiety about bequeathing and inheriting—and thus his need to
control his wife. But even in the midst of socialist
revolution this theoretical basis can provide the
underpinnings for an anti-feminist stance. And, as
we can see in history, it did. When Clara Zetkin,
German leader of the international socialist movement, interviewed Lenin in 1920, the trend of reaction had already been set in gear.

"The first proletarian dictatorship," said Lenin
to Zetkin, "is truly paving the way for complete
social equality of women. It eradicates more prejudice than volumes of feminist literature."[1] Here

56

Lenin simply confirmed Engels' prediction that socialist revolution, not feminism, is the necessary antidote to women's oppression; e.g., *socialist revolution makes feminism unnecessary.* Also take note of the switch in the socialist logic. Before the revolution, socialists reasoned that the problem was economic; after the revolution, it suddenly became a matter of "prejudice" to be eradicated—which is what this "unnecessary" feminist literature had aimed itself at from the start.

Indeed Lenin unabashedly criticized Zetkin for just about every aspect of "irrelevant" feminism undertaken by German socialist women. Considering the rage she must have felt about his negation of her activities, I find it truly amazing that she published this as she did. In the text she is subtle and discrete about what she herself was thinking while the great leader was speaking, so we can only assume its publication to be an act of courage. Nevertheless, I suppose this assumption to be accurate from my own experience as you might from yours. "What inspires your comrades, the proletarian women of Germany?" asks Lenin. "What about their proletarian class-consciousness? Do their interests and activities center on political demands of the moment? What is the focal point of their thoughts? I have heard strange things about that from the Russian and German comrades. I must tell you what I mean. I understand that in Hamburg a gifted Communist woman is bringing out a newspaper for prostitutes, and is trying to organize them for a revolutionary struggle. Now Rosa (Luxemburg), a *true Communist*, felt and acted like a *human being*, when she wrote an article in defense of the prostitutes who have landed in jail for violating a police regulation concerning their sad trade. They are unfortunate double victims of bourgeois society. *Victims*, first, of its *accursed system of property*, and secondly, of its *accursed moral hypocrisy*. There's no doubt about this. Only a coarse-grained and short-sighted person could forget this. *To understand* this is one thing, but it is quite another thing—how shall I put it—to *organize* the prostitute as a special revolutionary guild contingent and publish a trade paper for them. Are there really no industrial working women left in Germany who need organizing, who need a newspaper, who should be enlisted in your struggle? This is a morbid deviation..."[2]

Let me comment on what I see as the implications of what I have been describing. First, that Rosa, in acting like a true Communist, like a human being, was, to Lenin's satisfaction, not acting like a *woman*, which would have been despicable. Second, that to Lenin, prostitutes were clearly the victims of "systems and hypocrisy," not of *men*, the reified assumption of Engels' original thesis. Third, Lenin's admonishment that to understand the role of prostitutes is one thing but to work to change it quite another is a bit irrational—it directly contradicts Marx's own dictum that while the role of the philosopher is to understand the world, the point is to *change* it. By irrational, I mean a curious atrophy of Marxist beliefs and notions when the woman "question" arises. We will see how this tendency keeps growing.

"The record of your sins, Clara," Lenin goes on, "is even worse. I have been told that at the meetings arranged for reading and discussing with working women, sex and marriage problems come first. They are said to be the main objects of interest in your political instruction and educational work. I could not believe my ears when I heard that. The *first state* of proletarian dictatorship is battling with the *counter-revolutionaries of the whole world*. The situation in Germany calls for the greatest unity of all proletarian revolutionary forces, so that they can repel the counter-revolution which is pushing on. But active communist women are busy discussing sex problems and the forms of marriage—'past, present and future.' They consider it their most important task to enlighten working women on these questions. It is said that a pamphlet written by a Communist *authoress* from Vienna enjoys the greatest popularity. *What rot* that booklet is! *The workers read what is right in it long ago in Bebel."*

Notice the emphasis this time: in organizing discussions of sex and marriage, women are behaving despicably. Not only is their feminism unnecessary, it is destructive in detracting energies from the real struggle. That is, Lenin saw the urgency of the first proletariat state's battle with the counter-revolutionaries to be so great that women in another country (Germany) must not waste their time. The implication is, unfortunately, that discussion of sex and marriage must wait until the whole world is socialist or until there are counter-revolutionaries in none of it. Further, Lenin seems irrationally angry about the "rot" being published by a woman writer; in his rather curious view, nothing more could be said by women, about women, for women, than what had been written for workers by the male leader of

the German Social Democratic Party 40 years before. Women, then, don't need feminism, if workers
have proletariat dictatorships, or at least, male
socialist leaders?

I find these atrophies in reasoning so nonsensical and illogical that they become confusing. Emma
Goldman, walking the streets of Russia in the same
decade that Zetkin interviewed Lenin, discovered
similar disconcerting turns in socialist logic. Her
account of her disillusionment in Russia catches
some historically important shifts in reasoning. Before the revolution, as we saw, socialists blame the
system of property; afterwards, fault moves to defenders of the *previous system*. This shift is significant, because although already taken by 1920 it
holds on: Chinese indictment of Confucianism with
regard to women now reflects this same intellectual
buck-passing. Goldman wrote in her memoirs, "I
came upon a group of women, huddled together to
protect themselves from the cold. They were surrounded by soldiers, talking and gesticulating. Those
women, I learned, were prostitutes, who were selling
themselves for a pound of bread, a piece of soap or
chocolate. The soldiers were the only ones who could
afford to buy them because of their extra rations.
Prostitutes in revolutionary Russia. I wondered.
What is the Communist Government doing for these
unfortunates? What are the workers and peasant
Soviets doing? My escort smiled sadly. The Soviet
Government had closed the houses of prostitution
and was now trying to drive the women off the
streets, but the hunger and cold drove them back
again; besides the soldiers had to be humored. It was
too ghastly, too incredible to be real, yet there they

were—those shivering creatures for sale and their buyers, the red defenders of the Revolution. 'The cursed interventionists—the blockade—they are responsible,' said my escort. Why yes, the counter-revolutionaries and the blockade are responsible, I reassured myself. I tried to dismiss the thought of the huddled group, but it clung to me. I felt something snap within me."[3]

As I have said, this "snap" of Emma Goldman's is an important instant in the curious courtship of women's liberation and socialism. The pointing finger of blame rotates, as it always has. Before the revolution, the idea is that we should wait until after the revolution; after the revolution, the problems are left-overs from the past; then we should wait until socialism gets its feet on the ground, after the transitional period; next it is suggested that we should wait for a "higher stage" of socialist development; then we must wait until the day true communism arrives; well after the Chinese Revolution, Mao remarked that the problem of women would have to "ride" for maybe a thousand years.[4]

Time both replaces systemic planning to amend the wrongs and cancels out autonomous feminist organization. Yet it is hard to imagine how, to the revolutionary, time could be considered a strategy.

I can readily predict protests from some contemporary Marxist quarters: that to make much of these incidents is to magnify some small point of time way out of proportion, since the construction of socialism had hardly just begun. But, as we will explore, however one chooses to build a theory out of feminist realizations, one's evidence is brushed aside as unrepresentative. Moreover, I dwell on these encounters from this early period of Bolshevik history because facts, statistics, and positions drawn from later years are also brushed aside by yet other contemporary Marxists as not representative of the golden first few years of socialism before everything went astray. Yet, since so many practicing socialist concepts have been drawn from this point in time, the period *is* important for tracing the evolution of Marxist theory on "the woman question." After dissecting this juncture, we can no longer rest content with rote description of curious omissions and interesting coincidence, for the realization of the depths of socialist reaction to feminism brings with it an uneasy feeling of discomfort.

What was the nature of Emma's realization? In exploring the issue of what snapped in her mind, I would like to do two things: tie together several threads left hanging from previous sections in the text; and move beyond the level of relating socialist-feminist interaction. That is, I will attempt to *explain* the dynamic. Some of the cumulatively unsettling questions to be taken into account, in synopses, include: why does a feminist critique of socialist countries require such a justification? Why does disillusionment with socialism act as such a motivating force in the development of feminist theory? Why is there such a stalemate in the debates between Marxism and Feminism? Why do they take on such an abstract, polemical nature? Why did Marxist analysis abstract away from differences based on sex and age to project global class terms on the basis of interaction between two groups of fathers? Why has Engels' past and future argument served as such dogma in the Marxist tradition, when some would believe Marxism to be a *method* of critical thought, a realistic guide to political action? Why is contemporary socialist-feminism so quick to act in co-opting convenient components of radical feminism, almost in disrespect to the radically different assumptions? And why, in the left, are those radical feminist assumptions so frequently distorted? How can whole areas of women's lives be theoretically "left out" of analysis of an economic structure? Including the importance of women's economic contributions? Why did early socialist and feminist movements occur at the same time? Why is it so difficult to recover the contemporaneous aspect of those histories? Why did Engels look forward and backward for change, belittling contemporary feminist struggle? Why does this rotation of responsibility for examining the current order protract itself into a post-revolutionary trend? Why did Lenin so gleefully proclaim to Zetkin that feminism became unnecessary with the establishment of the dictatorship of the proletariat? And, even in questioning the inadequacy of the logic in traditional analysis, have we really explained why anti-feminist reaction grows, linked with the rise of socialist theory and practice?

The answer, as yet, is no. To accomplish such a comprehensive explanation, we must temporarily abandon the level of traditional political exchanges, that level of human *behavior* of which theory building is a part, and go deeper, to the level of human *motivation*. I deepen this critique to the layer of interaction between the *conscious* and the *unconscious* because I think, like others, that psychoanalysis can provide the missing link between the ideological superstructure (inclusive of politics and revolutionary theory) and the socio-economic base. An historian of the Marxist intellectual tradition once pointed out it was no accident that increased pessimism about the possibility of revolution accompanied an intensified appreciation of Freud's relevance. Since a parallel route occurs with feminism (an increasing pessimism that socialism can liberate women), I find myself propelled along the same turn. Others before me have as well; Mitchell and Rubin, for example, have already done theoretical work indicating the need to understand the unconscious structure of patriarchy. As we don't fully understand it yet from a feminist perspective, this path is slightly obstructed. Consequently, a radically feminist psycho-history of the interaction of socialism and feminism might seem premature—especially since Freud and the unconscious have such a poor reputation in the feminist movement, some of it deserved.[5] But if we don't take the risk of proceeding, I am left with the unpleasant task of recounting a depressing history, blow by blow, without a comprehending interpretation. I find that I can't simply drop the weight of this potential setback to the synthesis of Marxism and feminism on any reader's shoulders without offering some means to reduce the load. I hope to do this by simultaneously applying two sets of tools: those exercised in traditional political debate of revolutionary history, and those of Freudian psycho-history. The latter, less familiar in our milieu, exist in a tradition in their own right.[6] However, due to components understood as anti-feminist in other parts of this tradition, we are less accustomed to elaborating these conceptual devices on our own.[7] But by transcending this resistance, we will move in the direction of comprehending the shape of contradiction between the left's attitude and behavior toward women and feminism at different points in history. To make such a move is not to abandon the level of traditional political exchanges, as it might seem to do at first. For I believe that motivation is both conscious and unconscious—that an argument can be derived both consciously and unconsciously at the same time. As we know from common experience in the women's movement, many political arguments stem from personal anger and pain; and when socialism moves in the direction of justifying patriarchy (which is to say, to re-establish it) the question must be asked, why does this happen? What else is going on, unarticulated by the actors?

Footnotes

1. *The Emancipation of Women: From the Writings of V.I. Lenin,* International Publishers, New York, 1966, Appendix: "My Recollections of Lenin," (An Interview on the Woman Question), p. 98.
2. *Op. cit.,* p. 100.
3. Emma Goldman, *My Disillusionment in Russia,* Thomas Crowell, New York, 1970, pp. 11-12.
4. Cited in Richard Levy, "New Light on Mao: His Views on the Soviet Union's Political Economy," in *China Quarterly,* No. 61, March, 1975.
5. This is not the place to recount the feminist critiques of Freud, starting with Simone de Beauvoir and Betty Friedan, leading up to current, perhaps deserved, dissection, such as Florence Bush's "The Freudian Cover-Up: Child Molesting" in *Chrysalis,* Issue No 1, Vol. 1, 1977. Suffice it to say Juliet Mitchell has already traced this history in *Psychoanalysis and Feminism,* Pantheon, New York, 1974.
6. See, as an overview, Martin Jay's chapter on the assimilation of psychoanalysis in *Dialectical Imagination: A History of the Frankfurt School and the Institute of Social Research, 1923-1950,* Little Brown, Boston, 1973. Of this tradition, perhaps the books of Fromm and Marcuse are best known. Reich, at points in his career, made efforts along these lines too. Another introduction would be found in Paul A. Robinson's *The Freudian Left,* Harper and Row, New York, 1969. Then there is the current school, works written with psychoanalytic insight by other scholars, such as those by Philip Slater—*Earthwalk,* Anchor Press, Garden City, N.Y., 1974; and *Footholds,* Dutton, New York, 1977. See also *The Journal of Psychohistory,* a publication of the Institute for Psychohistory; and *Semiotexte,* particularly Vol. II, No. 3, 1977, a special issue devoted to discussion of Gilles Deleuze and Felix Guattari's *Anti-Oedipus,* Viking, New York, 1977.
7. However, this process is beginning. See Gayle Rubin, "The Traffic in Women", in *Toward an Anthropology of Women,* by Rayna Reiter, Monthly Review Press, New York, 1975; Nancy Chodorow, "Oedipal Asymmetries and Heterosexual Knots," in *Social Problems,* State University College at Buffalo, New York, April, 1976, Vol. 23, No. 4, p. 454-468; and Gertrude Lenzer, "On Masochism: A Contribution to the History of a Phantasy and its Theory," in *Signs,* Vol. 1, No. 2, p. 274-324.

PART TWO

Chapter Seven

Converging Theories on Stages of Revolution

I said that I was going to apply two sets of tools simultaneously to the same material, and pick up several of the remaining threads. Before we continue in the realm of traditional political concepts, let me define the other route which will be presented later to synthesize the material. An indication of what is meant by Freudian psycho-history, later to be put to use, seems necessary. I present it first so that you might consider its capability of filling in the missing connections.

Adorno, a European Marxist affiliated with the Frankfurt School which first attempted the integration of psychoanalysis and Marxism, once reflected that the most valuable insights from Freud were his exaggerations.[1] Toward the end of his life, Freud increasingly dared to exaggerate—to develop a theory of civilization and history based on a projection of his understanding of psychological stages in individual childhood development. From this, he saw projected the vicissitudes and dialectics of culture, society, and its growth, reasoning that the germ of one accounted for the shape of the other. He had always been interested in interpreting social as well as individual psychological events, patterns and problems. In books like *Group Psychology and Analysis of the Ego*, for example, he analyzed social institutions such as the church and the army as enlarged duplications of the psychological parts at war within the structure of an individual neurosis. But later on he took more of his courage into his own hands, perhaps hastened by the onset of his own death which made him realize he had less to fear of losing from the living. Perhaps he also did so to meet the challenge to understand the impending holocaust and mounting anti-semitism which forced him and others to take refuge in London. In this later period he wrote books such as *Moses and Monotheism*,[2] in which he tried to explain not only individual growth, individual psyche, and individual change, or conversely the neurotic bases for social institutions that seem embedded and hence static and ever-oppressing; but also the collective stages of struggle, the impetus to social change, the rationale for large upheavals.

As far as I know, nobody has picked up on these stages of humanity's development to specify the stages of revolution. Generalized Freudian concepts of revolutionary character and rebellious types have of course been made, glibly or not, depending on the political intent of the maker. As an example of the latter, Erich Fromm, a Marxist psychoanalyst who has written most widely for the general public, has said rather broadly that "the revolutionary character" harbors resentment toward authority figures;

but even in saying so, he pleaded that "the revolutionary character" should not be confused with those who might participate in rebellion and revolution at any particular historical moment. He intended this character sketch more as indicative of a revolutionary *nature*—one who might rebel not only in the field of politics but also in science, religion, theory and art.[3]

Rebellion has also been roughly characterized as revolt of youth against fathers. Rebels in turn have largely rejected this analysis, because it is demeaning to be told that one revolts against the encroachment of the Pentagon on campus because one was once thwarted by the father in the home; similarly, women have found it belittling to be told, while organizing marches about discrimination against women, that they suffer, really, from penis envy. Demeaning and belittling, of course, because these charges are usually used to discredit the movements, to stem their appeal. Demeaning and belittling, unless one comes to understand the depths of these psychological constructs operating in oneself—which I myself have been able to do only through the patient side of the clinical process—and then tries to turn the argument around to find in it a source of liberation and power. Instead of ridding oneself of intense unconscious "problems" and then "growing up" or "making adjustments" or "settling down" (which we know has occurred since the upheavals and mass movements of the '60's) might we not use psychoanalytic insights to ask further questions? This too is an available route. I remember once when I first began to study Marxism that I had been upset by a remark of a conservative university professor. In a School of International Affairs class at Columbia, he had said that the Third World was interested in Marxism and revolution only because the Third World was poor. I related this dismissal to one of my first radical friends, who answered with a guffaw, "so what!" and then proceeded to explain that the theory obviously appealed to those who had most reason to use it. Here I am suggesting we get to the unconscious roots of our problems, and use the theories which might explain them in a similar tactical vein. But to the degree that the concept of Oedipal rebellion has been used in analysis of revolution, it has usually been cast in terms of generations of young men vaguely angry at father, of resentful protesting male youth, i.e., of sons.

What, then, about the sexual dynamic of revolution? Can we merge the three historic paradigms? That of struggle between *classes* which we get from Marx; that of struggle between *generations* of men which we get from Freud; and that of struggle between men and women—between the *sexes*—as articulated by Millet, Firestone, Atkinson, and other radical feminists? With such an aim in mind, let's move on to the heart of this section. As we do, let us keep an insight of Fromm's in mind. His rationale for moving from the specificity of Freud's notion of Oedipal struggle was the tendency to extend the Oedipal complex to all human development, when in fact, he argued, it was restricted to patriarchal societies alone. A valid social psychology, he insisted, must recognize that when the socio-economic bases of a society changed, so did the social function of its libidinal structure. And when the rate of change between the two varied, an explosive situation might be created. I am not a social psychologist, but I am interested in articulating the material basis for revolution, both upheaval and result, socialist and feminist. So let us elaborate Fromm's proposition by deciphering the precise change in the socioeconomic basis of patriarchy which creates what we shall call, from the habit of history, a revolutionary situation. To do so we must block it out in stages.

Now to those who know the arguments of socialists, we have stepped on familiar ground by raising the notion of *stages*. So perhaps we should divest ourselves of some terminological confusion by examining the socialist stage concept first, and by doing so introduce some of the relevant factual material. When I mentioned before that women's liberation keeps getting "put off," to be solved with time, which is to say with gradual economic development, this was a muted reference to the theory of construction of socialism by stages.

This theory of construction of socialism by stages is exhorted not only for its supposed explanatory powers concerning women, but also with respect to other immediate problems which, at the onset of socialism and thus at the early moments of practicing socialist economic theory, are first described as *capitalist remnants*. These so-called remnants are to be tolerated at any present moment, theoretically to be dispensed with at another more prosperous time; and then secondly to be considered functional in the socialist context as they operate (though not admittedly) as necessary underpinnings to the socialist state; and then thirdly to be boldly identified as *socialist*.[4] The current Soviet concept of *socialist profits* illustrates such a theoretically disturbing culmination. Another illustration: by the time Stalin wrote *Economic Problems of the USSR,*[5] instead of maintaining the pre-revolutionary goal of abolishing classes, those in charge of the socialist state had contented themselves with the existence of "friendly classes." Hence, those aspects which the "stage theory" puts off for solution have a tendency to become incorporated as a basic component of the resulting new order. These characteristics are accomodated instead of gradually disappearing with economic development as was originally proferred. This happened, for example, with the notion of the gradually withering state of the post-revolutionary socialist future. The future came and the state was strengthened. The same phenomenon occurs with the theoretical treatment of gradual diminishment of the need for material incentives, hierarchical relations, and the unrealized liberation of women.

I mention other manifestations of the failure of the application of the stage concept, because I know how infuriating it can be to hear the argument only in the context of women. This is certainly possible, if one is not familiar with socialist literature on other topics, because the concept is so readily applied issue by issue with reference to women. This occurs, for example, when pre-revolutionary socialists are theoretically in favor of abolishing the family, and post-revolutionary socialists declare themselves proud of the "democratic united family." In the history of the Chinese revolution, this was certainly the case. The first few decades of the century saw the emergence of a militant feminist movement, of which space only permits a few glimpses here.[6] For example in 1912 a group of women surrounded the Chinese Parliament violently agitating for reversal of legislation concerning divorce. A writer prominent in the May Fourth Movement advocated the position that the sex and family revolution would have to occur before the economic revolution. In the first small rural Soviets beginning in the 1920's, legislation liberating women from marriage was among the earliest to be enacted; in one area thousands of divorces were reported to have occurred within the first few months of the legal adjustment. But after a brief Marriage Law campaign in the first few years following national liberation, coincidental with rural land reform which required the erosion of the family as a unit of property, the position solidified that a sound and durable family was necessary to build the socialist state. The same rapid transition occurred in the Soviet Union, where the first revolutionary years saw experimentation with free love, collective-living and communes; however, by the third decade of the first socialist country's existence, what Kate Millet called the "counter-revolution" had already set in. Legal abortion was abolished, and marriage laws and divorce codes tightened. We witnessed the beginnings of a theoretical rationale for this earlier with Lenin.

The major critique of the evolutionary stage theory to be made in light of this trend is that the act of "putting off" doesn't occur so easily. In fact it requires political suppression. Again, a few incidents to convey the feeling: during the United Front period of revolutionary struggle in China, the Communist Party based in Yenan reverted to a position of liberation of women solely through participation in production, apparently forgetting that participation in production was supposed to be the first step along a somewhat more liberating chain, leading to disintegration of the economic basis of the family.

Simultaneously, the party leadership condemned agitation around divorce, marriage, and sexual issues. Accordingly, leaders of women's organizations came on the carpet. Ting Ling, one of the leaders—and a revolutionary writer whose work could be considered in the contemporary light to be radical feminist—was forced to retract her famous "Thoughts on March 8th," in which she continued to "belabor" the stereotypic treatment of women, even at the hands of the comrades-in-struggle.[7] This necessity to suppress those who agitated around issues that were "put-off" indefinitely extended beyond the (some would say) predictable issues of marriage, sexuality and divorce. For example, Delia Davin, a British political economist, noted in her comprehensive book, *Women-Work and the Party in Revolutionary China*,[8] how this suppression extends to matters more traditionally associated with work. In the Chinese countryside of the 1950's, women's organizations struggled to separate accounting units for women's workpoints from those of fathers (for daughters) and husbands (for wives). It was believed that this tactical measure would force an equalization of pay, or true economic independence. Calculating workpoints by means of familial relations based wage differentials directly on sex and age characteristics, rather than on real contribution to productivity. (Nonetheless, reward to differently valued labor usually appears as the rationale for wage differentials in the socialist economic literature.) It is easy to see how this stabilized material basis for patriarchal kinship organization went hand in hand with the restraining political pressure against divorce by the party and the state. As Davin recounted, the economic struggle to unhook this familial calculation was lost or postponed until a later epoch, *not* for a specifically argued plan or strategic reason, but to be "temporarily" held in abeyance for a more prosperous period. The periodic abolishment of the national women's organization, for what is referred to as consolidation, is also a disturbing indicator of suppression, not comfortably felt as the natural evolution of the appropriate socialist stage.[9]

The theoretical rationalization for this postponement, now properly understood as suppression, was first articulated by Bukharin. Although others of his concepts were controversial and eventually rejected, his postulate of equilibrium, in an early book, *The Economics of the Transformation Period,*[10] provided the basis for the stage theory of socialist development. This was later to be codified in Stalin's thought. Basically, Bukharin dissected the process of socialist transformation into four stages, each distinguishable from the other by activities dominant at each point in the long term process. First was the era of *ideological revolution*, the pre-revolutionary period, when people began to question the existing order. Second was that of *political revolution,* the period of organization and upheaval, when the party formed itself and seized the state. Third was that of *economic revolution*, when the political power of the state was used to re-establish equilibrium, to create order out of the revolutionary chaos characteristic of the period of political transition. Fourth was that of *technological revolution*, when, developing from a re-established economic basis, development of productive forces was allowed to take charge and to raise the standard of living to such a degree that further adjustment in human relations—such as a change in belief—might have room to be made.

Now what happens to feminism in this schematized process? From this analysis, feminism is seen as appropriate primarily during the first stage, that of ideological revolution, when established patterns of thinking and believing about the old society are being overturned.[11] Thus, immediately after the revolution, Lenin openly showed his contemptuous concern that women not do anything to retard Russia's entrance to another stage, as the Soviet Union crossed the threshold from the second to the third, moving from primarily political to primarily economic concerns. And explicit contours of feminism became inappropriate as the Chinese revolution went from its primary ideological to primarily political phases.[12]

The question remains, *why?* Finding the socialist economic concepts on their own terms to be inexplicably flat, we will soon turn to the Freudian notion of stages for an explanation. But let us not proceed with such haste in our jump. Let me first explain that by "flat" I mean there is a lapse in the richness of thinking. As socialist struggle moves through its stages, a transformation of Marxist thought occurs; it loses its exciting, intriguing dialectic, and becomes scarcely more than nonsensical phrasing.[13] This atrophy is similar to that which occurs even prior to the revolution with regard to women. (For example, we noted earlier that if Marx foresaw change in the differential status of the sexes, we might expect Marxists to condone struggle in that arena, as Marx's notion of change was that it came about through struggle.)

Such atrophy in thinking historically has been associated with reformism in the socialist tradition. As we find nothing revolutionary in the socialist evolutionary concept of gradual automatic "growth" of women's equality, there is nothing revolutionary in the emerging socialist economic thought about development of a higher communistic order, piece by piece, separated process by separated process*— which only sheds light on the fact that *revolutionary* and *socialist* are by no means terms which should be considered synonymous. One might be socialist in aim but evolutionary in process, since even revolutionary socialists might advocate an evolutionary process when it comes to the aims of feminism. The emergence of gradualist thinking need not wait until after Bukharin's second stage; such a trend in political thinking might arise prior to the revolutionary step of seizing the state and hence replace the advocacy of such dramatic action. One thinks of the intellectual and political conservatism in the midst of German Social Democracy, culminating around the first World War.[14] As more of its leaders actually found themselves elected to seats in Parliament, backed by trade union power, they began to advocate the use of parliamentary reforms and bread and butter strikes as evolutionary strategy

---

* Maoism collapses these struggles, theoretically proposing that they might happen at the same time. Nevertheless, feminism remains within the structural division of "ideological struggle," whereas Chinese Communist literature hardly proposed that imperialism be defeated by "ideological struggle" with the Japanese. Moreover, feminism is categorized as a contradiction "among the people"—for example, between father and daughter; while the struggle between *father* and *father* (the Chinese Communists and the imperialists of Japan) is classified as a contradiction between two groups of *different* "people."

rather than as tactical steps leading to revolution. By the time of the Weimar Republic, during which they came to a tentative position of power, many had actually rejected the Marxist concept of violent revolution altogether. The leadership of the Social Democracy tried to maintain its own legitimacy by disassociating itself from bloody Bolshevik "excessess."

I have made a note of this because of the interesting process of exclusion of women—as leaders or as feminists—in both the evolutionary and the revolutionary tradition as either route puts some form of "socialist" into positions of leadership of society's institutions, rather than positions of leading resistance against them. As I mentioned before, women's and socialist organizations were thrown underground, and hence together, at the incipient stage of German Social Democracy during the Bismarck period. When the party had no power and it was in fact a legal risk to become a member, women formed a considerable proportion; as the party became more powerful, the internal position of women diminished.[15] Similarly, before the party's actual seizure of state power in China, women accounted for as high as 20 percent of the membership in some municipalities (few know that the founding of the Chinese Communist Party took place in a girls' school); but since national liberation, women have seldom reached even a 10 percent level of representation.[16] Furthermore, active women leaders find not only their feminism suppressed, but also their advocacy of "ultra-left" positions. For as male socialist leaders concentrate on the consolidation of power, women would-be leaders find themselves margin-

alized as unheeded voices of revolutionary consciousness (or, it might be said, *conscience*). Ting
Ling, for example, represented not only feminism in
China, but also the "left wing" Yenan writers who
resisted other conservatizing aspects of the '42 party
consolidation.[17]

One could also think of Rosa Luxemburg, that
famous political debater of whom even Lenin spoke
so approvingly despite the fact that before her death
she became his adversary. She wrote important
pamphlets such as *Reform or Revolution*, in which
she took the German Social Democracy party leadership to task for its encroaching co-optation; in her
final stay in a German prison, she wrote a pamphlet
criticizing the Leninist concept of proletarian dictatorship on behalf of the masses, which she warned
would co-opt decision-making by the masses. And
even in this, Luxemburg was only one of many
women in the Second International who doggedly
articulated and acted upon the "extreme" left
(or most revolutionary) position.[18] So, contrary
to Lenin's opinion, Luxemburg was "acting like a
woman," by her insistence on revolutionary purity
of the left. For it didn't make sense to many women to
put faith in parliamentary or trade union accom-
plishments. After all, being female, they could
neither vote (let alone get elected to parliamentary
seats) nor have a base for power in the trade unions
of mostly male membership. Unlike the leading
socialist men, they did not have the option of
stepping in to attempt the redirection of bourgeois
institutions towards socialist ends. This distance
gave them an acute perspective on the rising reform-
ist direction. Accordingly, with the outbreak of

World War I, women from the socialist parties all
over Europe gathered together to lead the Zimmerwald protest convention, which was provoked by the
majority moves in each of their respective parties to
cast votes for armaments in the Parliaments. In
Russia, Alexandra Kollontai took up a similar "ultra-left" position in leading the rank and file Workers Opposition to protest the consolidation of party
control.[19] And the parallels in Russia go back still
further.[20] When Russia's revolutionaries were in the
powerless position of resisting the Tsar, women
leaders resounded in famous name and number, be
that according to principles of the early terrorists,
the Narodniki, or the Social Revolutionaries. But the
female sex was diminished in the power structures of
the bolshevized institutions. The image of the Russian woman-as-revolutionary mutates from the Tsar-
shooting, young, bank-robbing woman, or the female character who rose at one of Dostoevsky's
famous exquisitely set dinner tables to speak against
"the family" (in *The Possessed*, also translated as
The Devils), to Katerina Breshkovskaia, posing in
great post-revolutionary portraits as Mother Russia.[21]

Although the history of the left shows women to
be gradually phased out with the passing of socialist
stages, post-revolutionary concepts continue to be
applied even in pre-revolutionary phases—concepts
arguing that no matter which stage we are in, we
should look to the next one. I have already referred to
this intensified stage-attitude about the question of
women in a pre-revolutionary situation—in Barnett's
notion that we should first abolish private property,

and then cross our fingers for the gradual dimish-
ment of rape and prostitution under socialism. Such
an unnatural application of the concept beyond its
reasonable extension is partly accentuated by the
pre-revolutionary socialists' temptation to borrow
concepts from successful revolutionaries or socialists further along in their practice. I find the result
curious, however, not only for the nonsensical conclusion. For this borrowing in itself violates the
socialist notion of stages: what is advocated in Stage
I might not be applicable or relevant until the arrival
of Stage III. Yet this obvious contradiction in logic
never causes the stage notion itself to be surren-
dered. The current position on women taken by the
evolutionist Italian Communist Party epitomizes
another problem with this process. In their concept,
progress for women is clearly delineated by steps:
Step I is that women will go into production; Step II
is that they will play a greater and greater role; Step
III is that they will eventually arrive at equality.

   All of this, of course, ignores the dialectic. Which
is: what if men *react* to women taking their first Step
I? After all, the bourgeoisie reacts to "slow" transition to socialism (or gradual accumulation of power
by workers through legitimate bourgeois channels)
with the violence of fascism—be it Hitler stomping
his heels on the ashes of the Weimar Republic, or
Pinochet's establishment of a military dictatorship
at the fall of Allende's Socialist Chile. Yet socialist
theory of the "gradual development of women's
equality" obscures the possibility of an analogous
form of reaction. For within the gradualist theory of
socialist stages, sexuality, male and female role

subversion, divorce, and liberation from marriage (whatever the current form) are seen as ideological factors. Their questioning is helpful in disrupting bourgeois order during the first stage of revolution, but only insofar as this disruption leads onward to the next stage of revolution, or evolution, depending on the precise historical moment. In the Freudian framework, however, sexuality and contingent issues (divorce, change in division of labor) cannot be stuck into the prevailing schema to be brushed aside at the next. For in the Freudian notions, sexuality forms the front-center home base for all other determinations, although the determination for social change has been articulated on a generational basis—as a struggle between male age groups, between fathers and sons.

Footnotes

1. Martin Jay, as cited in the last chapter: *Dialectical Imagination: A History of the Frankfurt School and the Institute of Social Research. 1923-50.* Little Brown, Boston, 1973.
2. See also *Civilization and Its Discontents, Totem and Taboo, Future of an Illusion,* to be referred to later in more depth.
3. Erich Fromm, "The Revolutionary Character," in *The Dogma of Christ and Other Essays on Religion, Psychology and Culture,* Holt, Rinehart and Winston, New York, 1963. Also elaborated in *Escape From Freedom.*
4. Raya Dunayavskaya (Trotsky's secretary at the age of 19 in Mexico) was, I believe, one of the first to pinpoint this process. See her December 1942 article in *New International,* "The Nature of the Russian Economy."
5. Joseph Stalin, *Economic Problems of the USSR,* International Publishers, New York, 1952.
6. Some of the most accessible accounts are in Julia Kristeva's *About Chinese Women,* Urizen Books, New York, 1977; Sheila Rowbotham's *Women, Resistance and Revolution,* Pantheon, 1972; Marilyn Young, editor, *Women in China,* Michigan Papers on Chinese Studies, No. 15; Margery Wolf and Roxane Witke, *Women in Chinese Society,* Stanford, 1975; *Signs,* Autumn 1976, Vol. 2, No. 1; and for those who would like to pursue the organizational forms striving to change women's position in greater detail, see also Charlotte Beahan, "Feminism and Nationalism in the Chinese Women's Press," *Modern China,* Vol. 1, No.4, October 1975; Virginia Chui-tin Chao, *The Anti-Footbinding Movement in China,* 1852-1912, unpublished Master's Thesis, Columbia University, 1966; Kuan Ch'in Chen, *Emancipation of Women in China,* unpublished Master's Thesis, Columbia University, 1933; Diane Betty Ostrovsky, *The Role of Women in the Chinese Labor Movement 1919-1927,* unpublished Master's Thesis, Columbia University, 1966. See also *A Short History of the Women's Movement in Modern Japan,* Tanaka Kazuko, Femintern Press, Tokyo, 1974 to compare to Japan especially in the early period when Chinese women students used to go abroad to study.
7. Available from Femintern Press, P.O. Box 5426, Tokyo, International 100-31, Japan, in pamphlet form (*Ting Ling: Purged Feminist*). Economic changes at this instant also bear some historical importance, especially in light of how the Yenan

period has been extolled as the cradle of Chinese communism, when it took on its specifically Chinese form, stressing such aspects as self-sufficiency and cooperation on the local level. Mark Seldon has mentioned in *The Yenan Way in Revolutionary China* (Harvard Univ. Press, 1971) how "caution was urged in the development of a movement for women's rights at this time in view of its potentially divisive effects," simultaneous with increased reliance on household industry in the area. As output from women's home weaving mounted in importance between 1938 and 1942, so did suppression of feminist struggle. "Walking on two legs" might be translated as "one foot in the home," meaning stabilization of the household, and cancellation of divorce struggle. Two sources which have reprinted Ting Ling's work (see above) cite Mao's "Talks at the Yenan Forum on Art and Literature" (in *Selected Readings from the Works of Mao Tse Tung,* Foreign Language Press, Peking, 1971) as part of a rebuke aimed specifically at Ting Ling and her ilk to silence their writing.

8. Delia Davin, *Woman-Work and the Party in Revolutionary China,* Oxford University Press, 1974.

9. The most recent mentioned in Norma Diamond's "Collectivization, Kinship and the Status of Women in China" in Reiter, *op. cit.* A sense of the long-term manipulation of the women's organizations in China can be found in primary documents collected by Elizabeth Croll in *The Women's Movement in China: A Selection of Readings,* 1949-73, Modern China Series No. 6, Anglo-Chinese Educational Institute, 1974, especially in the first section.

10. Bukharin, *The Economics of the Transformation Period,* Bergman Publishers, New York, 1971.

11. For a vivid example of the use of women's liberation as a tactic in socialist revolution, see *The Surrogate Proletariat: Moslem Women and Revolutionary Strategies in Soviet Central Asia, 1919-1929,* Gregory Massell, Princeton, 1974. Where cultural patterns were embedded so deep in the ethnic minorities, aspects of feminism interjected from above remained quite useful in political transition. Parallel analysis of China has been made by Kristeva (*op. cit.*) in the use of early marriage law campaigns to erode patriarchal economic familial units at the period of transition to the socialist state.

12. Judith Stacey, Dept. of Sociology, Univ. of California, Berkeley, is currently doing a dissertation on what she calls

the "Thermidorian Reaction" to family revolution in socialist countries. In her dissertation she will carefully trace and thoroughly analyze this process in China. See her "When Patriarchy Kow-Tows: The Significance of the Chinese Family Revolution for Feminist Theory," in *Feminist Studies*, Vol. 2, No. 23, (Spring '75). For Russia consult either Kent Greiger, *The Family in Soviet Russia*, Harvard, Cambridge, 1968; or Rudolph Schlesinger, *The Family in the USSR*, London, Routledge, Kegan and Paul, 1949.

13. This has been noted by those who have gone "beyond" the Marxist tradition (such as Wilhelm Reich in *Mass Psychology of Fascism)*, but not analyzed sufficiently within Marxism "proper."

14. See A.J. Berlau, *The German Social Democratic Party, 1914-1921*, New York, Columbia University Press, 1949; Julius Braunthal, *History of the Internationals, 1914-1943*, New York, Thomas Nelson and Sons, 1967; George Lichtheim, *Marxism: An Historical and Critical Study*, New York, Praeger, 1961; Carl Schorshe, *German Social Democracy, 1905-1917*, Harper and Row, New York, 1972. See also, for a very valuable specific case study, Mary Nolan's *The Socialist Movement in Dusseldorf, 1890-1914*, unpublished Ph.D. Thesis, Columbia University, 1975.

15. None of this, of course, is without struggle: neither the initial fight in, nor the marginalization. See Karen Honeycutt's "Clara Zetkin: A Socialist Approach to the Problem of Women's Oppression," in *Feminist Studies*, Spring-Summer, 1976, or her unpublished dissertation at Columbia, *Clara Zetkin: A Left-Wing Socialist and Feminist in Wilhelmian Germany* (1975). Or, to trace the historical dynamic in the trade unions: Hugh Puckett, in *Germany's Women Go Forward* (New York: Columbia University Press, 1930) mentions the anti-female sentiment expressed in the 1867 National Association of German Workingmen in Berlin (p. 275), to whom the ideal circumstances would be the return of women to the home. In *The Autobiography of a Working Woman* (London, Fisher Union, 1912) Adelheid Popp recounts her frustrating experiences being one of the earliest women workers to approach the German unions. Alice Henry, in *Women and the Labor Movement* (New York: Mac-Millan, 1927), recounts how, as the unions were established in an international structure, women workers were cast in a mute non-voting role.

16. For the earlier period, see Seldon, *op. cit.*, and compare to Heath Chamberlain's essay in *Elites in the People's Republic of China,* Robert Scalapino, editor, University of Washington Press, 1972. It is also interesting to note the steady climb of the median age of party leaders as the revolution itself ages.

17. See Yi-tsi Feuerwerker's discussion of Ting Ling's "When I was in Sha Chuan," reprinted in *Signs,* Autumn, 1976, Vol.2, No.1; and Gregor Benton, "The Yenan Literary Opposition," *New Left Review,* No. 92, July-August 1975, where Ting Ling's "Thoughts on March 8th" are also reprinted.

18. This can be seen by reading autobiographies of women active in the movement, such as Angelica Balabanoff's *My Life as a Rebel* (New York, Greenwood Press, 1968) or Toni Sender's *Autobiography of a German Rebel* (London: The Labor Book Service of Butler and Turner, Ltd., 1940). Curiously enough, Luxemburg's close ties with women and her female political identification, though large, is practically invisible to her male biographers, who primarily record her effect on men and her ability to compete on male terms (unless it is a crack about her size and looks). Robert Nettl's *Rosa Luxemburg* (London, Oxford University Press, 1966) is a prime example; P. Frolich's biography of the same name (London: Pluto Press, 1972), although written by an acquaintance, measures her on the same terms. Margaret Sanger's *An Autobiography* (New York, Dover Press, 1971), however, indicates that Rosa measured herself somewhat differently. She conducted a correspondence with Sanger throughout her political life. And Luxemburg mentioned in a letter to Tilde Emmanuel that she would like to be Penthesilea, queen of the Amazons who fought against the Greeks at Troy.

19. Lizzie Borden, in "Women and Anarchy" (*Heresies,* No. 2, May, 1977), has both noted this and placed it in the longer tradition, observing parallels more extensive in history than I have referred to here, such as during the Spanish Civil War. Unfortunately, the best analysis of Kollontai has not yet appeared in English—Ann Marie Troger's "Nachwort" to *Alexandria Kollantai: Die Situation der Frau in der gesellschaftlichen Ent Wicklung. Uierzehn Vorlesungen vor Arbeiterinnen und Bauerinnen an der Sverdlov-Universitat 1921,* Verlag Neuekritic. (Frankfort, 1975.) Short of

that, Louise Bryant's observations of the way in which Kollontai operated in the government bureaucracy (in *Six Months in Russia,* New York, Doran Co., 1918) is an interesting firsthand account. D. Freeley's "Women in the Paris Commune" (*International Socialist Review,* March, 1971) can further serve to internationalize this phenomenon, as can "Portugal's Most Militant Leftist Party, Led by a Woman," *New York Times,* October 14, 1975, p. 12.

20. See, for example, Barbara Engels' and Clifford Rosenthal's translation of memoirs, *Five Women Against the Tsar,* Knopf, 1975; Robert McNeal's "Women in the Russian Radical Movement," U. Mass./Amherst, History Department; and I. Steinberg's *Spiridonova: Revolutionary Terrorist,* London, Methuen and Co., Ltd., 1935.

21. See Alice Stone Blackstone, *Little Grandmother of the Revolution,* Boston, Little Brown and Company, 1917; or Katerina Breshkovskaia, *Hidden Springs of the Revolution: Personal Memoirs,* Stanford University Press, 1931.

Chapter Eight

Interaction of the Unconscious and the Conscious in Revolutionary Situations

We are at last prepared to pick up on the psycho-history line of the argument to see if sense can be made of the reported failure of socialists to maintain, in theory and in practice, their own notion of consistent progress toward women's liberation which, in their view, comes to replace explicitly feminist aims. As you will remember, this line of interplay between the conscious and unconscious is being unraveled for the purpose of defining the concept of feminist revolution. I remind you of this now to assure you that by doing so I am not asking you to uncritically accept all aspects of the Freudian tradition. Rather we will take from it what we can to use in the feminist interest. You will also recall that when discussing the contemporary context of socialist and feminist interaction we counterposed the Marxian notion of woman as laborer (wife is to the husband as proletariat is to the bourgeoisie) to the feminist notion of woman as property (womb is to alienated woman as means of production is to alienated worker). Now what can we learn from the Freudian tradition about the notion of woman as property? And how does the notion of women as property fit in with the Marxist notion of abolishing private property and centralizing its ownership in the state?

To embark upon this transition to the unconscious roots of *revolutionary situations,* I have found it necessary to make two adjustments in the concept of *revolutionary character* found in Fromm. First we will have to modify the notion of resentful *sons* who, as you will remember, Fromm identified as the rebellious actors. For while it is true that sons rebel against fathers, in the classical Freudian framework they do so in context of banding together as *brothers.* By emphasizing their mutual situation as brothers, their common experience as siblings, they transcend the dependent relation of son and take over the father's wife. A second necessary modification is to specify the general "resentment" that Fromm attributed to the revolutionary character in the aforementioned essay. That is, the resentment is traceable to jealousy for sexual privilege of the father over his private property, the wife. In this light, we shall examine some of Norman O. Brown's contemporary reflections on socialism and Marxism, before returning to Freud's initial historical application of his notions of incest taboo and Oedipal rebellion in *Totem and Taboo, Moses and Monotheism, Future of an Illusion,* and *Civilization and its Discontents.*

Brown tells us in his collected thoughts on the history of political theory that in Locke we witness the turn from espousing values of *fatherhood* or patriarchy (such as obedience to authority) to espousing the values of *brotherhood* such as were expressed in the French Revolution: liberty, equality among brothers, friendship, fraternity. Brown then returns to Plato to find a pre-capitalist, anti-authoritarian, anti-patriarchal position expressed in revolutionary situations. "In Plato," writes Brown, "the abolition of the family accomplishes the abolition of property: property is patriarchal, communism fraternal. So also in Marxism: Engels connected the family with private property and the state; society has been patriarchal and will become fraternal. Marxism, as a successor to Locke, picked up the cause of brotherhood. The history of Marxism shows how hard it is to kill the father, to get rid of the family, private property, and the state.[1] As Brown then points out, Freud directs us to the idea that the only true contrary of patriarchy is not matriarchy, but fraternity. The energy that builds fraternal organization, he notes, stems from rebellion against the family and the father and as Ortega y Gasset has written, from "youth preoccupied with women and resolved to fight."[2]

With Freud, then, let us examine the unconscious roots of this resolve to fight which culminates in the revolutionary situation, and connect these roots to the impending reaction to "gradual evolution" of equality for women which goes hand in hand with suppression of feminism and the re-establishment of a stable state after revolutionary upheaval. Again this phenomenon must be seen as the restriction of the revolutionary character of Marxist thinking when socialists as a group move from the stage of resisting established leaders to leading social institutions themselves—whether this occurs in still capitalist or in a post-capitalist context.

In the beginning, Freud wrote, there existed the primal horde which was dominated by the father. In this original human community, the father dominated all women—his daughters and wives were his own sexual property, tabooed for his sons. The sons of the father took refuge on the outskirts of the community. Banding together, they took solace among themselves. They feared the wrath of the father, for each had sexual longings for the only female objects, the daughters and wives. Each desired to become the father as well. The brothers returned to the community, killed the father, and divided his daughters and wives up among themselves. Since they acted in concert, they each consoled themselves with not becoming the sole exclusive primal father. This consolation comes with the building of a family, each brother his own. The individual patriarchal family replaced the primal patriarchal horde community. The brothers adjusted themselves to this out of guilt for murdering the father, although a struggle for rights of succession begins shortly afterward. And in human history we see the rise not of a primal father, but of God and then king.

Although Freud intended this fable to explain the epochs of civilization, he applied it in a slightly variant form to smaller pieces of society and history. In his research on the origins of totemistic religion, he observed the same stages of incest taboo which provoke Oedipal rebellion in a condensed progression. Except that whereas in the primal horde fable the father is actually killed by the brothers, in the totem religion the brothers kill the father-substitute—an animal which is then worshipped as a relic, symbolically enshrined on a pole. After the murder, the animal is consumed in a feast and brothers suffer remorse. They experience guilt for having acted out of unconscious desire to kill the father, though it was only an animal that they actually organized themselves together to slay. This guilt, arising from ambivalent feelings to both *be* and *kill* the father, induces a mass projection of a new father to whom the brothers can be even more obedient in compensation for the murderous act. This is the rise of monotheistic religion. Patriarchal values hold sway, such as obedience and submission. This forms the basis for rising social institutions constructed along a patriarchal, ruling-father model,* for the remorse is not sufficiently appeased by intensely held beliefs in the father; this requires real and actual structural submission as well.

How then do these Freudian myths contribute to our understanding of revolution? In each case, whether the patricide was symbolic or real, the brothers become the father. Some become *more* like the father,

---

*I mean this specifically in the sense that each sex and age grouping is assigned to a patriarchically-ordered role. Other definitions of patriarchal institutions have been more broad, but still aptly characterize the emerging party structure. Sheila Collins, for instance, writes, "Patriarchal institutions tend to be ordered along hierarchical chains of command, or lines of authority, rather than being communal or anarchic; they are exclusive rather than being inclusive, and are goal-directed rather than maintenance-oriented."

becoming patriarchs in the new social institutions; others become *less* like the father, in that out of guilt for the instinctual murder they obey the new patriarchal order with great religious fervor. Yes, this is a speculative chain of analogous reasoning. But there are many graphic illustrations: the Chinese masses waving the *Little Red Book*; the huge posters of Stalin, Lenin, and Marx that adorn every Cuban factory. This symbolic worship of the new father also finds its material, structural base in the social institutions which re-establish the patriarchy on a more stable basis. The individual patriarchal family is re-established, first of all, for the majority of fathers; and furthermore the minority of fathers reign over the new patriarchal institutions—chiefly, the party and the state. The state being the enlarged property unit which replaces the individual property unit of the family, also structures itself, via its head, the party, to control an enlarged group of wives. Ho Chi Minh once remarked that the party was like a family, as quoted in Arlene Bergman's book on *Women in Vietnam*,[3] in her discussion of strict adherence to a familial structure in a more contemporary revolution. The analysis of the party's enlarged reproduction of patriarchal family organization can be specified a great deal further than that.

As the proletarian party takes the form of consolidation of *brothers* into *fathers*, the new fathers organize their wives through the women's organizations.[4] China is an example. The wives of Central Committee members have often sat in high positions in the women's organizations; they have served as leaders in the (powerless, figurehead) People's Congress as well. Or look at the Puerto

Rican Socialist Party structure in New York City where a wife of a Central Committee member heads the Women's Commission.

Fathers have not only wives; they also have daughters. What happens to daughters in this newly emerging patriarchal political structure in which, like in the family, the father is at the head? Initially daughters are incorporated into the organizations of communist *youth* just like their brothers. But we should not allow the term "youth" to mislead us; the "youth" of different sexes have different futures in store. Brothers may step across the line to become fathers; but daughters face a future as a powerless wife. One month after Mao died, his wife was removed from her position on the Politboro and condemned viciously as the leader of "the Gang of Four"—which, however one reads politically, can also be read as another instance of the powerlessness of a woman who rises not on her own but through bonds with a man. Chiang Ching is now (in 1978) becoming the scapegoat for everything currently identified as a left-wing "error" in China over the last ten years. The Bad Wife preserves the sanctity of the name of the Dead Father, who remains all good. We know what the future of the powerless wife means in the patriarchal structure of the family; in the political structure it means that brothers move up and on to the active membership in the party; daughters take on the role of wife in the women's organizations.

This, then, is the structure. What about the dynamic of struggle?

As the larger coordinating political institution takes on its patriarchal form, autonomous feminism (or freedom for women from wifedom) is forced out by the tightening contours. This requires suppression of the daughters: Alexandra Kollontai, Ting Ling. These daughters are not only daughters in their commitment to feminism, in their fight against the reduction of the political role of women to that of the party-father's wife, but the daughter's militancy extends to other issues. For example, I mentioned that Alexandra Kollontai advocated workers' control; that Rosa Luxemburg was against reformism and for revolution. This historical chain of "ultra-left" women leaders fights against the transformation of brothers into fathers, either in a still-capitalist or in a post-capitalist context. The pain they feel parallels that which forced a snap in Emma Goldman's head as she realized she was watching the brother comrade step into, or justify, the authoritarian father role. The pain is that of abandonment and loss—the ultimate daughter's desertion.

Gradualism, slow transformation by stages or pieces: whether the plan of the dictatorship of the prole-patriarch or the parliamentary proposals of the British Labor Party and the Italian Communist Party, this voice of reformism that emerges from the midst of the socialist movement is the voice of the father, not the voice of the brother. Allegiance to revolution remains the voice of the daughter. The voice of the wife, one must realize, is not her own, for through her speaks the father.

But surely by now you are anxious for some illustration. Let me give you that in the voice of Angelica Balabanoff, another heroic daughter who made the implicit feminist critique of Bolshevik patriarchalism in her book, *My Impressions of*

Lenin.[5] Listen to her describe a confrontation between a wouldn't-be-wife (Zetkin) and Lenin, five
years before the famous interview we examined
before. She is writing about the left-wing, largely
female, Zimmerwald movement, which protested
cooptation by the leading Second International fathers during the First World War:

> It was necessary, first of all, to give tangible
> expression to the faith in internationalism
> that animated us, to carry our voice to the
> greatest possible number of war victims,
> and to give this endeavor a collective, polit-
> ical character without arousing the impres-
> sion that a new international was in the
> making.

> It was not long before I received letters from
> various countries protesting against the
> war, affirming faith in the International,
> and voicing the necessity for a renewal of
> contacts among comrades in various coun-
> tries. One of the early attempts to renew
> faith through active women, and the first in
> which both Lenin and the Bolsheviks partic-
> ipated, took place in Switzerland since it
> was impossible for the men to leave their
> countries in wartime. The concrete proposal
> came from Germany through the pioneer of
> the International Socialist women's move-
> ment, Clara Zetkin. With her I arranged the
> clandestine meeting in Bern, March 1915.

> As soon as the plan had matured, the Bol-
> shevik Central Committee in Switzerland

notified us that Lenin's wife, and another Bolshevik woman of the old guard, would participate as delegates. From that day the Bolsheviks, with Lenin and Zinoviev as their spokesmen, became the most eager supporters of our initiative. At times their interest in the women's movement had an almost comic aspect; for a man like Lenin to sit for days on end in the corner of a coffeehouse where the women delegates of his faction came to report everything that happened at the convention and to ask for instructions was, no doubt, ludicrous.

There was continuous coming and going. The slightest modification of a resolution, the meeting was interrupted to allow the Bolshevik delegates to hear Lenin's opinion.

One of our chief tasks was to write a manifesto to shake the masses overcome and silenced by the war, carry to them the voice of solidarity among the peoples solemnly reconfirmed at an international meeting of mothers, wives, and widows, the most atrociously striken war victims. We wanted it to be known that socialism was not dead and that the International, whose functioning was temporarily suspended, survived as belief, as conviction, as a shining ideal. Having at last found a formula suited for an appeal to all the women of the proletariat and having obtained the consent of the majority of the delegates, we were confronted with the Bolshevik women's refusal to sign our manifesto. They demanded the passing of a resolution which the other delegates had rejected because of the implicit obligations. The minority group proposed the formation of a new International. The delegates to the Bern meeting did not consider themselves in a position to decide on matters of such importance without having heard the opinions of their respective parties.

The Bolshevik women—cornered by the objections and exhortations of the other delegates who begged them not to wreck the convention, for if one single signature were missing the meeting would have failed in its aim of showing the unanimity of the delegates of all the countries regardless of the "block" their governments belonged to—did not dare to make any concession and left to confer with Lenin. These interruptions were filled with tension and anxiety.

Clara Zetkin, the president of the convention, was pale, very nervous, and suffering from a heart disease; she did not succeed in controlling the situation. The irritated and discouraged delegates were ready to leave without reaching the goal, though they had overcome innumerable difficulties to participate in this convention, which was intended as, and succeeded in being, the first spark of light in the deathly dark of war.

The negotiations and the long talks between the Bolshevik delegates and Lenin did not yield anything; they merely drove most of the delegates to the brink of exasperation. The session was interrupted, and Clara Zetkin went to Lenin to make an attempt at breaking the deadlock. Hours passed in anguish and pain.

Lenin and the president of the (women's) convention came to a compromise...

Encouraged by the example of the Socialist women and aiming at the same goal, several members of the Socialist youth gathered a few weeks later in the same locale, the House of the People. Their participation in an international convention was of even greater significance than ours, partly because their going to Switzerland in wartime involved greater risk than did the attendance of women.

Guided by the same objectives, the Bolsheviks presented the same agenda at the youth convention, causing confusion and despair...

That the leading prole-patriarch dominates over youth as well as women should be brought to mind by the hold of Lenin's entitlement of his book: *Left-Wing Communism, an Infantile Disorder.* He speaks here in the voice of the chastizing father to his disobedient, upstart children. And his anger in the interview with Clara Zetkin quoted earlier stemmed from the fact that the prole-patriarch's enlarged group of wives refused to behave as the proper disciplining mother, futher extending his command. "Nowadays all thoughts of Communist women," he continued to chastize this leading socialist woman, "or working women, should be centered on the proletarian revolution, which will lay the basis for, among other things, the necessary revision of material and sexual relation... I was told that sex problems are a favorite subject of our youth organizations, too, and that there are hardly enough lectures on the subject... You must fight that too. There is no lack of contact between the youth movement and the women's movement..." To be coordinated, it seems, through the proletarian movement, the party, the organization of the fathers.

Lenin next infers, through the use of the possessive pronoun, that communist women are the prole-patriarch's property. *"Our* Communist women *everywhere* should cooperate methodically with young people. This will be a continuation of motherhood, will elevate it from the individual to the social sphere."[6] The changing role of women in socialist revolutions, then, can be surmised: at Stage I, we have the rebellious daughter; by Stage II, she has become the obedient wife, disciplining the children on behalf of the father. Either that or she is expelled.

You will recall, from our first identification of the patriarchal component of Marxism, evidence to support the notion of the rise of capitalism as a long term process whereby the economic power of one group of fathers was transformed by that of another group of fathers. The accumulation of capital by the dominant patriarchs—the capitalists—partly came

about by their access to the labor of the disenfranchised patriarchs' women. Think, for example,
that the first factory workers in nearly every
emerging-capitalist situation are peasant daughters, whose fathers are in the old mode of petty com-
modity production, back in agriculture, or on the
farm, where the individual patriarch's household is
the dominant unit of production.[7]

Engels, writing on *The Condition of the Working
Class in England* in the 1840's over a quarter of a
century before he turned his critical faculties to
exploring the oppression of women, reflected on the
anger provoked by the capitalist's overturning of the
accustomed patriarchal familial positions. He might
well have remained with his earlier observation. As
he wrote, of the 419,560 factory workers in Great
Britain, 242,296, or over half, were women. "The
employment of women at once breaks up the family" he complains, "for when the wife spends 12 or 13
hours every day in the mill, and the husband works
the same length of time elsewhere, what becomes of
the children? They grow up like weeds... The employment of the wife dissolves the family utterly and of
necessity, and this dissolution, in our present society, which is based upon the family, brings the most
demoralizing of consequences for parents as well as
children. The children who grow up under such
conditions can never feel at home in the family
which they themselves found, because they have
always been accustomed to isolation. In many cases
the family is not wholly dissolved by the employment of the wife, but turned upside down. The wife
supports the family, the husband sits at home, tends
the children, sweeps the room and cooks...It is easy to

imagine the wrath aroused among working-men by this reversal of all relations within the family, while other social conditions remain unchanged." Engels adds, "We must admit that so total a reversal of the position of the sexes can only come to pass because the sexes have been placed in a false position from the beginning. If the reign of the wife over the husband, as inevitably brought about by the factory system, is inhuman, the pristine rule of the husband over the wife must have been inhuman too."[8]

However rationally Engels could step outside of history to understand this, his astute intellectual distance does not hold sway over the depths of unconscious rage which the ruling patriarchs have set into motion among the disenfranchised fathers' strata. In Lenin's remarks to Zetkin, we witnessed the culmination of the struggle this sparked for reassertion. Short of revolution, the rage could be channeled more concretely and directly. For example, the working-men Engels depicts did go on to organize trade unions, to demand protective labor legislation for women and children, and to regain their patriarchal position in the family, although the individual patriarch's family was no longer the locus of the production system.

Although articulated on the level of protective legislation, this is only the surface reflection of the rage which has been loosed, which, if pushed too far, will culminate in socialist revolution. On the conscious level the fact remains that this initial articulation promotes a superficial solidarity with feminism: women are being mistreated. Only later does this become confusing, since the feminist and socialist motivation for observing, and hence interpreting, the same phenomenon differ greatly. That of the socialists is motivated by the disenfranchised fathers' sense that their property rights have been violated. Apparently in some bursts of consciousness, Marx noted this as well, for example, in the section on introduction of modern machines in *Capital.* Yet these observations have never been incorporated in the whole body of non-feminist Marxist theory, which took such a divergent direction. The force behind the Marxist recognition is a sense of outrage, and this sense leads to the constant use of woman to illustrate the epitome of capitalist, not patriarchal, exploitation. In *Karl Marx on Education, Women, and Children,*[9] Saul Padover has compiled a compendium of such examples. The cumulative effect must be recognized as being unconsciously severe, and perhaps could be understood with reference to a piece of non-socialist history. America was incited to call for the U.S. entrance to the Spanish American War by the sensationalist news accounts of the rape of a woman.

Throughout left literature on many subjects, then, "woman" appears most often as powerless victim. She is used to illustrate the strength of the socialist cause, which, although in selection is unconsciously motivated, unconsciously incites hatred, disgust and anger at the all-empowered capitalist (the bad, un-protecting, violating father). The Latin America and Empire Report, NACLA, serves as a prime example: "Exploitation in Nicaragua," as was published in the February 1976 issue from an interview with a woman militant in a national liberation struggle, "is *epitomized* by the rural woman who cuts coffee or cotton. Along with her older children and perhaps her own parents, *she* is left with the least desirable and lowest paid tasks. Nicaragua's minimum wage laws are never enforced in the countryside; *she* earns a fraction of the amount earned by a man for the same back-breaking labor. Since the work is seasonal, *she* must maintain a tiny plot of land—or migrate to a nearby city to find work, mostly as a maid. *She* may be brought to the city as a 'daughter of the house,' a virtual slave, below even the regular maids, paid nothing for doing the hardest housework. Or *she* may find her only work opportunity as a prostitute, serving the whims of the Guardia Nacional."[10]

In view of the Freudian notion of the rebellious brother horde incited in Oedipal rage by the sexual privilege of the tyrannical primal father, the following step in my argument will come as no surprise, though I will not quarrel with you if you are at this point reluctant to take it, as I have had to step outside of history to fully come to this realization myself. It is indeed ironic that a revolutionary movement which superficially allies itself with concerns of feminism does so in protective indignation. The notion of unconscious appeal to violation of patriarchal property rights of the disenfranchised fathers has somewhat clarified our vision. But the sexual connotation of this appeal could sharpen our insight a great deal further.

Consider, for example, another excerpt from the current left publication, NACLA. The issue under consideration is exploitation of Puerto Rico by organized crime:

> Part of the entertainment the Ferre's Hotel Berinquen offers to attract guests is a girlie

show presented every Wednesday in the Cloud Room.

Master of Ceremonies: Let's see, Evelyn, are you wearing panties today? Come here, let me see. Ah! Evelyn is a good girl. Come, show these gentlemen, Evelyn isn't wearing panties. Sandra. Again without panties? Good. Good. Sandra likes to walk around without panties. It's lots of fun, right, Sandra?

After nearly an hour of watching the women, sometimes with panties and without bras, other times with bras but without panties, the master of ceremonies announces that the first part of the show is over.

Then the nude women come out and amble among the tables where the wealthy executive clientele is eating, seductively displaying, among other things, the most poetic part of the woman.[11]

Norman Holland, in a psychoanalytic approach both to reading and writing,[12] points to the fact that non-fiction is just as much a revelation of the unconscious as fiction but in a more sublimated form. While he does so by going to the lengths of analyzing the structure of sentences, grammar, and meter, I will be content enough to ask you to notice the *content* of the illustration. Does this nearly pornographic nature of a piece of left propaganda reveal unconscious furor at the *greater* (more powerful, capitalist) fathers? If, in this example, the projection remains safely obscured (after all, they are just reporting the "facts"), let us turn to more directly revealing material.

Think, for example, of *Lady Chatterley's Lover*. D.H. Lawrence was a socialist as he wrote it; and in early drafts the game-keeper was active in a local left wing political cell. Doesn't this game keeper force the mine-owner's wife into sexual submission? Or, consult Mary McCarthy's portrayal of male socialist characters in *The Group*. Particularly insightful is the lecture of Harold, the socialist actor, delivered to Dottie, the daughter of a capitalist in the import business, about "the brief struggle" in which his rising class would seize the state. Another of the female characters, originally living with an impotent socialist, marries a rich banker, bears his son, and moves uptown. The theme—the disenfranchised father's anger at the supra-father's greater control of their own daughters and wives—is even more explicit in a manuscript of a novel I was recently allowed to read by a young socialist writer, Shawn Bayer. His novel begins as a young lawyer working for a corporation bursts into a board meeting and holds up the directors with a gun. The young employee remains there until his message has been aired on television: that his wife and daughter were recently killed in an unnecessary accident, because the cars put out by the corporation hadn't been sufficiently checked for safety prior to consumer delivery. Finally, the theme of jealousy for the "bad-father's" greater access to women was last brought home to me when a I saw a left wing labor history play about the shirt-waist fires in early New York. All of the garment workers were women. Every night as they left the factory they were fondled by the "bad father," the capitalist, or by his young male-hireling who as the audience knew, would someday take over the firm. This fondling, sure enough, created the effect of inducing both sexual jealousy and protective anger. But the pivotal scene occurred when the fire burnt down the factory where the women worked and they died. I have never seen a left play where a group of working class *men* were portrayed as hopelessly trapped and captured. Granted, this occurred in history, but the point is, what has the left lifted up to become part of its culture? And then during the final scene, as the women writhe in the flames and die, they take off their outer brown garments to reveal see-through sheer white gowns. The image of victimized sexual object is certainly instilled in the mind.

Having established the point that, consciously or unconsciously, the socialist concern with women stems from the same source of sexual jealousy that motivated the primal horde to its Oedipal rebellion, let us move more directly to periods of actual revolution, as our intent was to discover the unconscious roots of the revolutionary upheaval, the revolutionary situation.

Let us make this move with the help of Agnes Smedley, a writer who spent several years in China during the revolutionary upheaval. Having undergone psychoanalysis herself before she went, her writing is rich with insightful Freudian observation. This should be considered with another observation, made by Kristeva in her book *About Chinese Women,* (also psychoanalytic), that a constant motif of the literature of the May 4th movement and the

1930's revolutionary Chinese literature is that of the revolt of sons against fathers.

To Agnes Smedley, there is a flow between feelings of hate for one's father and the strength of one's dedication towards ending the entire system. She writes of young revolutionary men pining in jealousy for their father's concubines. "I hate this man called my father," one of them says. "Our families are a great load dragging all us youth down to the bottom of the sea. I know so many young men ruined this way. You may say we deserve it or we would rebel. In my native village, they do not even know how to rebel; it is not we who are to blame—it is the system."[13]

Some of the men from whom she provoked such intimate confessions were furious at their fathers' privilege of buying second wives—at the emotional expense of the original wives, or the mothers. One such, whom Smedley described in a 1930 *New Republic* sketch, "Five Women of Mukden," unwittingly allowed Smedley to witness a dramatic indicative scene of the son's protest of his father's purchase of a "singsong girl of 16." "My little hostess," writes Smedley, "does not dare object. But her eldest son is a modern student in long black flowing robes, and he objects. He has told his father that he leaves home, never to return, the day he takes a second wife.

" 'You are a son...You will act like a son!' his father informs him."

"But the son is impious and clear-minded, and a week ago his father struck him across the face. They say Chinese sons love their fathers. Not the sons I have known. Never have I seen more hatred in the eyes of a man than in those of this eldest son of my hostess. He speaks little before a guest, but his eyes speak when they light on his father. There is constant friction between them.

" 'In the olden days,' the father boasts to me, 'the daughter-in-law had to stand while the son's parents ate.'

"The son breaks in: 'That is why so many of them died!' "

I mention this conflict between fathers and sons over treatment of wives and daughters because I feel, like Smedley, that this sexual politics had a great deal to do with the revolutionary upheaval. Like the sensitive journalist she was, she made an apt record not only of things that women did, which in itself would be an important historical contribution, but also of how men reacted to the subversion of the traditional position of women. Sons saw eroding, right in front of their eyes, the kind of power exercised by their fathers over women; the conflict provoked by this dynamic underlies the ambivalent relationship between feminism and the revolutionary movement, culminating in the crack-down on autonomous feminism later on.

On this note, let us return to Fromm's idea that a change in the libidinal structure might create a volatile situation, if that change were "out of kilter" with the socio-economic configuration. We might accept a part of that notion although in doing so we turn the idea on its head. For the change in material conditions itself upsets the libidinal structure, which provokes the volatile, or revolutionary, situation. Although class exploitation occurs over time, these particular conditions provoke the revolt.

I have documented in another article how the

primary earning capacity of the adult male head of the household in China was infringed upon by the invasion of foreign capital. Foreign capital accumulation was achieved at the expense of the agricultural sector, where the population lived and worked in patriarchal households, by drawing other family members out of the house for employment—particularly daughters.

Combining this change in the material base with the Freudian idea of Oedipal jealousy for the dominant fathers' territorial rights over women, the unconsciously-motivating factor for socialist revolution comes to the fore. The ruling-fathers' super-exploitation of the disenfranchised fathers' wommen—be that in factories where the danger of sexual encounter lurks, or beyond—provokes the disenfranchised fathers to revolt. They are rising in fact as the primal-hoarding brothers.

Thus, the historical coincidence between the rise of feminism and the emergence of revolutionary movements no longer seems accidental, unaccountable-for, strange. The dictionary defines "coincidence" as a remarkable occurrence of events, ideas, etc., at the same time, in a way that sometimes suggests a causal relation. Here I am suggesting that the same conditions which allow for the development of feminism provoke a socialist reaction.

Hence, the Marxist distortion of feminist positions, the concealment of coincidental feminist history from the socialist view, and the abstraction away from differences based on sex and age to focus on the role of the father can only be described, in sum, as a mammoth blocking.[14] So deep is this phenomenon that I know I must return with care to history to support the point. For although the statement is primarily disturbing on a psychic level, since it requires one to give up faith in an illusion, to restructure what one wants to believe, it will be repelled by the accusation of not being based on fact; for that is the easiest route—dismissal.

This defensive response, taken on some levels before the argument has been fully contemplated (if perhaps not by you, then by another reader), will be easy to maintain—since, due to what I have named as the nature of the problem, much of the necessary history to support this does not enjoy great parlance in the public view. Although I argue this case on the basis of my extensive research on the history of China, there are parallels in other revolutionary situations. I must share some of these to convince you that this is indeed a historic trend, not limited to only one specific case.

I was persuaded again of the expansive application of the argument by seeing a revival of a Broadway play, *Fiddler on the Roof,* set in pogrom-torn pre-revolutionary Tsarist Russia, portraying the human experience of Jews in a small ghetto town. This experience is uniquely explored through the point of view of the individual family members: mamas, papas, daughters and sons. In the opening scene, each kin grouping, gathered from all the Jewish families throughout the town, stands together to explain their position in chorus. Subsequent scenes explore the trials of life of each social group. In one of the early scenes where we are with the papas, a young male student meets the milkman, Tevya, at the well. The young man offers to become a tutor to the oldest man's sons. The student explains that children should be taught about unfairness, property relations, and the accumulation of wealth in the hands of a few, where it should not remain for long. Tevya replies sadly that he has no sons, only five daughters. Undaunted, the young student shows eagerness to instruct Tevya's daughters as well. With this flamboyant statement the youth provokes a violent reaction from the formerly silent rabbi sitting with Tevya at the well. "Watch it," he raises his head to warn, "he's a radical!" Later, the same student leads the way in over-turning the long tradition of sex-segregated dancing. Then, as rumors of encroaching political upheaval spread, the town matchmaker turns to the audience to announce, "and that's what comes from men and women dancing!"

Although only an incidence of popularized folk culture, there might be a grain of truth in how the matchmaker sees the world: changes in the sexual division of labor provoke chaos throughout the social order.

My journalistic experience in Chile during the government of Socialist Allende led me to share the matchmaker's perception of the sexual basis for political disruption. I occupied myself there doing photos and stories about women. Thus I had an opportunity to see first-hand the changes in women's economic roles. One of my assignments was to make a comparative profile of working class families. I spent most of my time on this story visiting homes in a suburban housing project. In most homes which I visited, the male head of the household was unemployed. In one, the wife supported the household by raising rabbits in the backyard. Her teenage daughters also contributed to the household from jobs found while enrolled in a secretarial school. In another, the wife supported the household by setting up a beauty parlor in the front room. In a third, the wife supported the family by taking in laundry and going out to wash clothes.

Later I was able to corroborate with statistics these impressions that working class women in the pre-revolutionary situation had moved into the primary earning role.[15] Brazilian sociologist Michelle Mattlart found, in her study of lower class Chilean women in the late 1960's, that 56 percent continued to work after marriage. They did so either because the head of the household was unemployed or because his earning power was insufficient: many women were the sole support of the family. Other studies have pointed to the changing sexual division of labor which was occurring, both in the city and the country, over an extended period. Still others have documented the change in attitudes of women at the time: 62 percent were in favor of women's participation in the labor market; 54 percent affirmed that household tasks and child care should be equally the responsibility of wife and father in the home. And yet of all the women interviewed, only one wife had succeeded in coralling the domestic assistance of the head of the household at home.

Years later and well after the coup, I interviewed some of the leading Chilean socialist women for North American radio. I asked if they thought this changing economic division within the working class household created tensions which fed in any way into either the revolutionary or reactionary process. Their answer at the time was no. Yet one of the guests on the program, Carmen Gloria Acquire, in 1971, had been put in charge of the new Ministry of Women and the Family. This ministry was criticized at the time by some North American observers as more of a play for votes than a sincere attempt to change the immediate situation of women. This was especially remarked by those who pointed out that Allende, in promoting the ministry's institution, discussed "woman" almost exclusively in her mother role, in the nuclear family function.[16]

But why, given the real changes in working class household structure which I have already described—changes which propelled the woman to increasingly outstrip the father in his primary-earning capacity? Perhaps the government's approach was consciously or unconsciously a reactionary appeal to the more conservative nature of the working class men, who *wanted their wives back, as mothers, in the home*, and who desired to become the primary bread winners once more. This suspicion was graphically confirmed for me when I visited the southern town of Valdivia. There the winner of the "Best Woman" contest on the socialist radio station had been chosen because she raised 13 children!

Elevation of motherhood was one of many reactions to women's strides; another took the form of vicious ridicule of the short-lived proposal to draft women, along with men, into national service. The government's proposal was that women should give a year of service as voluntary, unpaid paraprofessional workers in health and education. Part of the opposition's campaign against this move, which could be construed as an attempt to consider women and men equally, was a series of posters and magazine articles showing scantily-dressed women toting grenades and rifles.

My visits to the agrarian cooperatives in Valdivia hardly dispelled my belief that this "general" class struggle (which I now see clearly as the struggle of the fathers) would gradually improve the situation of women, as I was told by various leaders of party commissions on women. In one cooperative, the jobs of women had actually been replaced as the peasant-fathers' cooperative began to take over aspects of dairy production with the government's newly-imported machinery. I say the cooperatives were in reality organizations of peasant fathers. I spent many weeks roaming the countryside in Chile trying to find a woman who participated in the collective governing structures of the appropriated farms, but I could find only one, and she was a cooperative member because she had taken over her husband's accounting tasks on the farm when widowed. She herself complained to me that the invitations to government training sessions, where the *compañeros* would learn to operate the new machinery, were addressed to the men, not to the *compañeras*. Once, she explained, she had made an effort to involve women in the meetings of the cooperative fathers' community. When she, a lone woman, brought it up for a vote, the response was made that the women could not come because they were home with the children. I suggested that she might propose the tactics of Lysistrata (witholding sex unless the men stayed home at least one night, or unless, perhaps, for one night only, one man babysat with all the children so that wives could come to vote), but she thought I was joking. The same woman explained to me how she was hurt by the negligence of Santiago housewives to notify peasant women about the notorious "pots and pans" march against food shortages. Aghast, I asked why; I had been told those marching were all reactionary bourgeois women. In exasperation, she explained her response: these economic times were especially hard on women, as they all had to cook with scarcely any food in the house. And remember, this is from a member of an agrarian peasant cooperative!

Perhaps I have allowed my reminiscences about Chile to lead me off course, but it has struck me that the same change in the material basis which has been thought of as a precondition for feminism— which theoretically gives women a basis to wage a struggle for independence—can also, curiously enough, serve as an unacknowledged impetus for the development of a socialist movement. The move of women towards independent or primary earning status does upset the household. Yet before a feminist movement has time to successfully carry the progress of women further, a radical movement dominated by men generally develops, setting the sexual division of labor "right" again.

The conversation with this peasant woman in Chile was vividly brought to my mind again when I visited a farmworkers' cooperative in California. As I sat with a mixed group of socialists, most not as feminist as I, I asked a series of questions: "Are all the members of your cooperative men?" "Yes, just the head of the family comes to the meetings." "And does each member of the family receive a wage?" "Well, the wives who do the clerical work here don't get paid, because it isn't really working." "What about the actual division of labor on the farm?" "Each father has his wife and children harvest his section during the busy season." "Doesn't the wife get paid money of her own?" "No, it's calculated in the head-of-the-household account."

The disturbing effect of this unexamined "natural" phenomenon overcame me again, when, back in New York, I heard James O'Connor, a Marxist economist, lecture. Keynoting a conference on dialectics at N.Y.U., he traced the rise of the early socialist movements. I saw immediately how this was linked to the disenfranchisement of fathers who had been self-employed in crafts. Brecht's play about the French Commune, O'Connor said, represented the trials and tribulations of small craftsmen who were losing their shops. Each indeed was protesting, as well, what O'Connor called the "feminization" of the labor force: while the craftsmen were being deprived of their small shops by larger factory competition, the capitalist factory owners were busily employing women. O'Connor identified this mechanism as an early source for American unions, which, begun in the craft trades, supplied the basis for the early twentieth century American socialist movement. James Weinstein noted the second phase of this observation in his *Decline of American Socialism*; feminist political economist Heidi Hartmann, in a recent article in *Signs*, noted the first: how the male trade unions and craft organizations grew in response to disruption of traditional sexual division of labor with the rise of capitalism. Further, Hartmann notes that as factory production became established, the males used their labor organizations to limit women's place in the labor market.[17] Thönnessen perceptively called this "proletarian anti-feminism" in his account of the social democratic unions in late nineteenth century Germany. O'Connor went on to remark that such a reaction to "feminization" provided the basis for current farmworkers organizations as well. In California the growers have begun to use machinery which displaces fathers and employs a growing number of women. In this light, then, it is more clear how the farmworkers' fathers' co-op I had visited had been, though probably unconscious, an organized reaction to the growers' increasing employment of women.

What is more disturbing is that all this fits only too well with what I have learned about China: that the primary earning capacity of adult males (fathers), when undermined by the invasion of foreign capitalists (the bigger fathers), was reasserted after the socialist revolution—and patriarchy regained its material footing.

Not to chastize the Chinese, however, it seems that many revolutionaries do likewise when revolutions are examined for long-term historical trends. Papers presented at the 1976 Wellesley Conference on Women and Development, for example, documented how the labor force participation of women, rising rapidly before the Congolese liberation, rapidly stabilized and began to decline after the success of that revolution. And Susan Brownmiller, in *Against our Will: Men, Women, and Rape,* has blown the dust off the archives to show how much mass rape of the "bigger" (white, colonialist) fathers' women was part of the celebration of Lumumba's forces—which can be seen as only the start of the no-longer-disenfranchised men putting *all* the women back into their historic places.[18]

But what about current situations? A woman who grew up in Malaysia told me that the recruitment of women on the part of the multinationals has led to a male anti-multinational revolt; that their daughters and/or potential wives should not be seduced to the cities by the multinationals is the feeling. The multinationals do bill themselves as female liberators—this is the attraction. The factories even offer the women modern (western) culture classes. The women workers begin to wear miniskirts. They resist returning to the villages. At Hilton Hotels they attend company sponsored dances. All this is impetus for male revolt in defiance, euphemistically known as protection. No small wonder then, that in closing her commentary on the papers on patriarchy and class at the American Economics Association, Heidi Hartmann has asked, "To what extent are national liberation movements embodiments of male resistance to multinational corporations seeking women's labor as they invade the Third World?"

To the extent that this question is even asked, the sand runs through the hour glass and Engels' analysis has reached its final hour. Obviously class analysis ignores the dialectic: fathers of the disenfranchised class react against that first step (into production) taken by their own daughters and wives who become free play—though paid labor—for other more powerful fathers.

So, having convinced myself beyond a doubt about its necessity, I will move through the steps of a creation of categoric analysis to evaluate the change in women's position. Needless to say, the sole tactic derived by class analysis—getting women into production—is simply not enough. I will pull apart and put back together the socialist and feminist arguments about women in socialist countries, particularly China. Lest you forget, I am still seeking the necessary change in economic relations which we might enact after seizing the state and collectivizing the material wealth of productive property. Tracing this psycho-historical line of argument has only convinced me of the need to be well-prepared. Working with theories of unconscious motivation, we have just derived political categories. We found daughters, fathers, brothers and wives each acting as distinct social groupings in political situations. Now we shall return to the conscious level to derive economic categories through this investigation of the socialist and feminist positions concerning the role of women in socialist countries. In the end, the result will be the production of political-economic categories operating on both conscious and unconscious levels.

Even in this return to the conscious level of political discourse, it is important to bear in mind the dialectic between the conscious and the unconscious. The interaction between the two holds the force of persuasive power even in these debates which we shall unwind in order to examine. For the historical fact that socialists and feminists have arrived at such loggerheads in these debates does not stem only from a simple "failure to understand each other." The need to sustain a belief in a protective father—be that Marx or Mao—underlies the resistance to acknowledge what is and what is not "there," what is and what is not likely to happen with regard to women in a socialist country.

Freud wrote in *Group Psychology and Analysis of the Ego* that the socialistic tie seems to be taking the place of the cohesion that religion once provided.

Yet in *Future of an Illusion* he was excited about the liberation that the death of religion would create. Religious beliefs, he said, promoted an intolerance for those outside the group; with the overcoming of the need for intolerance would come the dawn of human liberation. In a brief discussion on the beliefs of the communists, he despaired: "If we do away with personal rights over material wealth, there still remains prerogative in the field of sexual relations, which is bound to become the source of the strongest dislike and the most violent hostility among men who in other respects are on an equal footing. If we were to remove this factor too, by allowing complete freedom of sexual life and thus abolishing the family, the germ-cell of civilization, we cannot, it is true, easily foresee what new paths the development of civilization could take."[19] My only desire is that this derivation might make such a foreseeing easier.

Footnotes

1. Norman O. Brown, *Love's Body*. Vintage. New York, 1966, p. 8.
2. *Op. cit.*, pp. 13-14.
3. Arlene Bergman, *Women in Vietnam*, People's Press, San Francisco, 1975.
4. Nadezhdas Drupskaya's *Memories of Lenin*, written by his wife, provides interesting material (International Publishers, New York, 1930); as does Roxane Witke's *Comrade Chiang Ching:Mao's Wife Self-Revealed*, Little Brown, Boston, 1977. The latter book created quite a fury as much for the wife's speaking ill of the father as for reflecting poorly on the defenseless dead. Yet even the language of left mythological literature reveals the historical trend in capsule form. Orville Schell and Joseph Esherick, in *Modern China,* Vintage, New York, 1972), write of Mao leading the Red Army in a manner similar to that with which Moses is written about leading the Israelites. And about women they add: "Among the 100,000 in the Vanguard were 35 women, including Mao's pregnant wife." (p. 87) While recently attending a seminar of the U.S.-China People's Friendship Association, the extent to which this develops did not fail to pass my ear. "Even Sun Yat Sen's wife," I was told, was discovered in the Cultural Revolution to be materialistic. I asked if this remarkably symbolic woman had a name. I was met with a guffaw and a stifled grin from across the table. The left and the right have this viewpoint in common, as can be seen in this *New York Times* article, "Analysts Study Wives for Clues on China's Leaders," Sunday, March 12, 1978:

   In China, where the public appearances and rank accorded leaders' wives are often as significant as that given their husbands, analysts are studying the treatment of several prominent women at the National People's Congress that ended last weekend in Peking

   The wife of Teng Hsiao-ping, the often controversial Deputy Prime Minister, attended the Congress as a delegate from the army, as did her husband.

   Analysts consider the army an unusual choice as a constituency for both Mr. Teng and his wife, Cho Lin. Although Mr. Teng is chief of staff of the armed forces and spent his early career as a political commissar in the Red Army, Peking would have seemed a more likely constituency, the analysts say, and therefore having the Tengs represent the army seems to reflect Mr. Teng's strong support by the military.

Although 503 of the 3,444 delegates to the Congress, China's nominal legislature, came from the army, 10 of the 26 members of the Communist Party Politburo were from the armed forces.

Speculation on Her Job

This was the first time that Cho Lin, who is about 70 years old, had been identified as a member of the army and her position is not known. There is speculation that Mr. Teng might have installed her in the army's General Office, which handles sensitive communications. The former Defense Minister, Lin Piao, who reportedly died in a plane crash in Mongolia in 1971 after trying to assassinate Mao Tse-tung, put his wife into that post.

Another well-known woman, Lin Chia-wei, the wife of Li Hsien-nien, the fourth-ranking member of the Chinese heirarchy, attended the congress as a deputy from Peking.

At the same time, Tsao Yi-ou, the widow of Kang Sheng, the longtime head of China's secret police and a close associate of Mao, appears to have been demoted. She was elected a deputy from Peking, but she was not named to the slate of officers on the Presidium. At the previous National People's Congress in 1975, when her husband and Mao were both still alive, she was a member of the Standing Committee.

The Chinese press agency, Hsinhua, also disclosed recently that a 43-year-old woman who is a former textile mill worker, Hao Chien-hsiu, had been appointed a deputy minister of the textile industry. The ministry was re-established only last month after having been abolished in the Cultural Revolution.

Miss Hao, who was also elected to the party Central Committee last summer, appears to be a public replacement for another famous woman textile mill worker, Wu Kuei-hsien. Miss Wu rose to membership in the Politburo but has disappeared, presumably because of ties to the radicals.

5. Angelica Balabanoff, *My Impressions of Lenin,* University of Michigan Press, Ann Arbor, 1969, p. 39-42. And here is a more contemporary example taken from the early stages of the recent revival of the women's movement.

THE COMRADES AND WOMEN'S LIB
CORINNA ADAM
New Statesman—19 November 1971

There came a point, during the proceedings of the 32nd Congress of the Communist Party this week, when I felt sure the next speaker would say, 'This is, after all, a family party.' It was such a respectable occasion, notably lacking in the frivolous hangers-on and entertaining eccentrics to be found at the other party congresses. People chatted over thermoses and cheese sandwiches during the very brief lunch breaks at Camden Town Hall, or went out with their relations for fish and chips. A far cry from the excesses of the Brighton Metropole. It amounted to a noteworthy occasion when the General Secretary, John Gollan, took a few fraternal delegates out to the spaghetti parlour round the corner.

Which is perhaps as it should be. Certainly the Congress afforded some revolutionary moments, for instance when the black fraternal delegate from Detroit embraced the fraternal delegate from South Vietnam, and tears sprang to the eyes of a lady warrior from Ireland, grown white haired in the struggle. But for most of the time the atmosphere was extrememely British and correct. A family affair in more than one sense. And it was in their attitude to that most entrenched of bourgeois institutions that the majority of delegates showed how far from revolutionary all but their economic aspirations are. There they sat in the hall, row upon row of solid, decent, hard-working family men: kind, no doubt, to their wives and proud of their children. But men is the operative word—of 422 delegates only 70 were women.

Yet it was the women who made the most interesting contribution to the debate. Only the *Morning Star* covered it. The rest of the reading public got what they always get in stories about the Left—reports of schism and attacks on the leadership. But this year, the women did provide something else. The party's new heretics are its young female members. It is they who are now defying the dogma—by saying, in this case, that as far as the Women Question is concerned, the CP is no longer in the vanguard.

'Women in Society' was one of the major resolutions before the congress. To set it on the agenda at all was a triumph for the young militants, most of whom were not even born when the last resolution dealing specifically with women was passed in 1938. There are ideological reasons for the long gap. Since it is a received truth across the left wing spectrum that women are equal to men, it theoretically follows that it is wrong (or as a Marxist would put it, unprincipled) to make women a special category. Not that this has ever prevented a left wing party from forming a women section. Not that it means that in Camden Town Hall the men were making tea, issuing passes, taking up collections: as at any other conference, the boring work was done by women, huddled together in little groups in a way the comrades would find offensive, if the people concerned were black or under-age.

The resolution itself was a compromise. It called, piously and expectedly, for more nursery schools, equal pay, job and educational opportunities, more women readers of the *Morning Star*. But it did also mention the Women's Liberation Movement, if only *en passant* and after considerable struggle between the drafters. Usually (although the British CP congress is a good deal more open than many) the speeches only afford occasional glimpses of what is going on behind the scenes. This week, for instance, one had to listen between the lines to understand the basic disagreement over the Irish Question. The executive position is somewhat more cautious that that of the *New Statesman*: phased withdrawal of troops, proportional representation in elections, implementation of necessary reforms. Some of the speakers wanted immediate withdrawal, and were rebuked for ultra-leftist adventurism, but no one openly supported the IRA (which is seen, I think, as 'opportunistic'). There is little doubt where most comrades' sympathies lie, but no one says so out loud.

The women, however, actually shouted their disapproval of the official line. Their open dissension was interesting not only as such, but also as the clearest example of what many observers think is happening

in the CP at the moment—that the younger members
want official sympathy for the various radical groups
growing up around the country, but would like to learn
from them rather than corral them within a party
structure.

'Jumbles, bazaars and equal pay' was how a young
woman from Birmingham, Jackie Atkin, defined the
party's view of woman's role. Communists needed to
understand the basic Women's Lib message that
women were oppressed in a different extra way that
didn't apply to men. A way for instance—and here she
stumbled over her words—'that makes us inartic-
ulate.' The mainly male audience loved her, for stum-
bling. She had proven herself vulnerable, i.e., feminine. Oh dear.

A delegate from Cornwall got up to reply, and proved
exactly what the younger woman meant. 'While you
men are reading the *Morning Star,* we are doing the
washing up.' And her solution? That the male comrades should read bits out of the *Star* to the female
comrades engaged upon household chores. Another
member of the old guard, Jean Styles of Streathem,
produced the old line that 'if you educate a woman you
educate a family'—always one of the most dangerous
arguments for the education of women, since it leads
them straight out of the laboratory into the needle-
work room. She compounded this by criticising the
Women's Lib demand for 24 hour nurseries (which,
among other things would release women as well as
men for political work) on the grounds that 'this is
really something that should be decided within the
family.'

Family, family. 'Housing, rents, fuel, education, peace
and now school milk,' said a *Morning Star* journalist,
Beatrice Campbell. All worthy causes, but what had
they to do specifically with women? Why should
women be especially concerned with peace? And why,
come to that, were there so few women at the congress.
Why no creche? Applause. But, sure enough, there
were well-trained older women to tell us a) that we
cared more about peace because of our maternal
instinct, and b) that most real mothers preferred to
stay at home. The 'you are unfeminine' attack is
always launched most strongly by women against
women. In this case it was done by the formidable
Betty Reid, who declared that nowhere in Women's

Lib literature had she found any real reference to the needs or rights of children (really?) and moreover, no one would want to bring small children 'from a distance, to some corner of this building.' Loud cries of 'oh yes, we would' from different parts of the hall.

After which a man summed up for the national Executive. The theme of sexual liberation was not new, said Gerry Low with a note of rebuke in his voice. It had been much discussed in the early years after the Russian Revolution. Women's Lib was either non-political or ultra-leftist. It was 'so far removed from the thinking of ordinary people as actually to hold back progress.' Back to the family. Back to the hearth. Back to the struggle as we know it. And the militants will stay, presumably, to fight another round.

After it was all over, a Russian acquaintance said: 'what I find so extraordinary is that these young women belong to the Communist Party in the first place. I think the leadership would be crazy to let them go. But, you know, perhaps they want a quiet life!'

6. "The Emancipation of Women," from *The Writings of V.I. Lenin*. International Publishers, New York, 1966, p. 104.
7. See Jean Scott and Louise Tilly, "Women's Work and the Family in Nineteenth Century Europe," in *Comparative Studies in Society and History*, Vol. 17, No. 1, pp. 36-64; and for the U.S., Rosalyn Baxandall, Linda Gordon, and Susan Reverby, *America's Working Women*, Vintage, New York, 1976.
8. Quoted from *Karl Marx and Frederich Engels on Britain*, Foreign Language Press, Moscow, 1953, pp. 176-179, in Hilda Scott's *Does Socialism Liberate Women*, Beacon Press, Boston, p. 31. I suggest the reader find the source there in order to contrast our discussion.
9. Saul Padover, *Karl Marx on Education, Women, and Children*. McGraw Hill, New York, 1975.
10. *NACLA's Latin America and Empire Report,* Vol. 10, No. 2. Feb. 1976, p. 3. In the familiar expression used by protesters at rallies, "Up against the wall mother-fucker," the rage is expressed more directly, incited by the historical remnants of jealousy of the father's sexual privilege over the wife.
11. *NACLA's Latin America and Empire Report*, Vol. 6, No. 6. July-August 1972, p.17.
12. Norman Holland, "Prose and Minds: A Psychoanalytic Approach to Non-Fiction," in *Victorian Prose as Art*, George Levine and William Madden, Oxford University Press, New York, 1968.

13. These excerpts are from Jan and Steve Mackinnon's selec-
    tions of Smedley's writings about China, in *Portraits of
    Chinese Women in Revolution,* Feminist Press, Old West-
    bury, 1975. In *Daughter of Earth,* Smedley's autobiograph-
    ical novel also reprinted by Feminist Press, one also has a
    portrait of a rebellious daughter who withdraws from
    political activity temporarily of her own choosing; though
    under great pressure she was not technically being expelled.
    In that volume, she writes how her comrades reminded her
    overwhelmingly of "father" and "brother." Her difficulties
    in the Indian National Movement did arise when she
    violated the role of "political wife." From this specific
    instance perhaps readers can get a feel for how the cate-
    gories might apply to more familiar political situations.
14. This is not the proof, but it is the position: from *Portrait of
    Marx,* by Werner Blumenberg, Herder and Herder, New
    York, 1972, trans. Douglas Scott, p.16:

    > The mother was not very well educated, but she was a
    > woman with very warm feelings who was entirely
    > absorbed in looking after the family. The son could
    > expect no intellectual stimulation from her... When he
    > was a student his mother sent him lots of good advice,
    > although it gave her a great deal of trouble to write in
    > German. For example, in November 1835: '...you must
    > not think it merely a weakness of our sex if I am
    > curious to hear how you have established your tiny
    > household, and whether economy takes first place in it
    > as it must in all households large and small, and here
    > I must say dear Carl that you should never look upon
    > cleanliness and order as a trivial matter since your
    > health and spirits depend on it, make sure that your
    > rooms are scrubbed out often, keep a regular time for
    > it—and wash yourself every week my dear Carl with
    > soap and sponge—how do you manage with coffee, do
    > you make it yourself or what, I beg you to tell me
    > everything to do with housekeeping, I only hope your
    > beloved muse will not feel insulted by your mother's
    > prose for I can tell you that humble things help one to
    > attain the highest and best, now if you wish for
    > anything at Christmas that I can give you then I shall
    > be happy to do it, so goodby my dear dear Carl, be a
    > good boy, think always of God and your parents, your
    > loving mother Henriette Marx...'

    With maternal pressure such as this, isn't it understandable
    why her son would block out all theoretic concern for the
    household?

15. Batya Weinbaum, "The Story of Eladia and Isolina: Old and New Approaches to Family Planning in Chile," UNICEF *News*, No. 74, January, 1973; Armand and Michelle Mattelart, *La Mujer Chilena en una Nueva Sociedad*, Editorial del Pacifica, Santiago, 1968; Patricia Garret, "Some Structural Constraints on the Agricultural Activities of Women: The Chilean Hacienda," paper presented at the Women and Development Conference, Wellesley, 1976.
16. See Katherine Ann Gilfeather's paper also presented at the Wellesley Conference: "Women: Changing Role Models and the Catholic Church in Chile," and Elsa Chaney's "Women in Latin American Politics: The Case of Peru and Chile," in Anne Pescatello, ed. *Female and Male in Latin America*, University of Pittsburgh Press, 1973, for the supermadre notion of women in Chilean politics.
17. O'Connor is author of *Fiscal Crisis of the State*, St. Martin's Press, New York, 1973; Weinstein's *The Decline of Socialism in America, 1912-1925* was published by Monthly Review Press, New York, 1967; and for Hartmann see "Capitalism, Patriarchy and Job Segregation by Sex," in *Signs*, Vol. 1, No. 5, Part 2, pp. 37-69.
18. Susan Brownmiller, *Against Our Will. Men, Women, and Rape,* Simon and Schuster, New York, 1975.
19. Sigmund Freud, *Future of an Illusion,* Anchor Books, Doubleday, Garden City, New York, 1964.

PART THREE

Chapter Nine

Socialist and Feminist Arguments on Women in Socialist Countries

Part I: The Comparative Reference: To Men or Women, Where and When?

The socialist argument tests the progress of women in socialist countries by two cross-sets of comparisons: the group of women *now* in a given socialist country is compared alternatively to the group of women in the same country *before* the revolution and to groups of women outside that society in other, completely different, capitalist societies. We opened with an example of the first comparison: that of *women now* to *women then*. There might be a few women on the Central Committee *now,* Barbara Ehrenreich said when speaking about China, but *before* the revolution female infanticide used to be a common practice. An example of the second yardstick is the common comparison between women in the Soviet Union and women in America, or between women in China and women in India. The best of these comparisons control for levels of economic development, but some don't. For example, the isolated housewife of highly industrialized urban North America is often compared to the active, community-oriented housewife in China, who through her neighborhood organization serves the people. It must be admitted that this most methodologically-suspect form of comparison has been encouraged by radical tourism in socialist countries, a pursuit actively promoted by the left.

The feminist reasoning proceeds from the principle that either of the above sets the frame of reference askew by comparing women in one society to women in another society taken out of the historically specific context. The feminist argument moves the frame of reference to *men within that society:* comparing numbers of men to numbers of women on the Central Committee, or getting comparable figures for educational structures, high army posts, better-paid jobs. Feminist analysis usually stops at this point where it becomes clear that men and women are not equal so no further comparative references are established.

But what about a combination of the yardsticks? For either is by itself insufficient. While socialists look backwards and outward or forward, feminists tend to look at the present without historical continuity. To resort to formulae for posing a solution: how about *women then/men then* versus *women now/men now*? By this I mean: we might establish a method for comparing the relation between men and women over time, instead of only at the present moment like the feminists, or instead of looking only at two groups of women in different historical periods as do the socialists. For example, socialists often say that women were feudal slaves before the revolution in China. This is not enough, unless it is known what the men were doing: maybe the men were slaves too. Briefly reconsidering the phenomenon of pre-revolutionary suicides committed in protest of arranged marriages, we might get a hint of new material that such an approach is bound to surface. Mao wrote an essay in 1919 pitying the plight of a woman who took her own life rather than marrying;[1] the essay is frequently referred to now with emphasis on the horrors women were saved from by national liberation. But this formula for analysis would lead us to other information: Agnes Smedley, the American journalist there at the time, observed that men committed suicide to get out of arranged marriages as well. Smedley also observed that men were sold into slavery, shipped around to work on wage-labor farms, or brought up as cheap labor to be exported to other countries.[2] Socialist literature concentrates on the slave-like existence of women, as if to remove this comparable information about men from the lens as we focus. The point is that we should look at both sexes historically as well as at the present moment.

It might also be helpful to establish various locales for applying the comparative formula. Previously I mentioned that socialists compare women in socialism to women under capitalism: the Soviet Union has more female doctors, for example, than does the United States. If we are to compare cross-systems of economy, it seems necessary to do so with more of a method. Looking at any socialist country in this century, we are really confronting the period of emergence of a new mode of production; so let's compare this scenario to the years of emergence of capitalism. Rather than seeing how a fledgling socialism compares to a grown-up capitalism, let's compare it to the beginning of capitalism. The sense of this suggestion might be fathomed by reflecting how the formative years of childhood determine the basis for adulthood. Sex role analysis might further refine the analogy: to understand men and women, we must examine the comparative experience of boys and girls. To give meaning to this extended analogy, return to the Central Committee reference. As we ask if a woman has ever served on that organ of state power, we might ask if there was ever a queen in sixteenth century England. You might protest that to compare a monarch to a committee is to compare a football to a basketball when you want to look at the players. But in the course of these incongruities, our goal will be accomplished: to comprehend the relation of men to women in two different systems.

This combined standard of evaluation will allow a more thorough pursuit of both the past and the present. We want to examine history to uncover the mechanisms of change, not simply to "compare the present to the past and see progress," as is the habit of practicing socialists and those who visit their countries—in this case the Chinese as quoted by an American health expert, Ruth Sidel.[3] This complicated project requires more than the recounting of horrors from the "bitter past." The project is to see why a society develops and how it transforms itself. One must look at how old forms are negated so as to give rise to new developments.[4] Instead, the socialist argument has used history simplistically as if to de-legitimate the feminist counter-criteria of comparing women to men as "ahistorical." A prime and early example of this was the response of Nancy Milton (socialist) to Janet Salaff (feminist) published in *Socialist Revolution.*[5]

After saying that "the emancipation of China's women, whether judged *in the light of their own historical advance, or in comparison to women of other countries* is a miracle of social change..." Milton goes on to berate Salaff for her brevity in discussing traditional China as a place where women were denied participation in political institutions. "This is truly a marvel of understatement," Milton continued with her criticism, "to describe a social, political and economic institution—the traditional family— which, for over a thousand years, by means of an ethic both personal and official, denied women all legal, economic, social and personal rights. The right to the choice of a husband (in a system in which marriage was the only means of economic survival), the right to divorce, to remarriage if widowed, to their own children, to education, to property, to un- crippled feet..." *ad infinitum.* Salaff told me private- ly, years after the heat of this argument had hooked me on unraveling the strands in the polemic, that she herself was confused by the virulence of Milton's reaction. Taken in another context, the absurdity of this simplistic misuse of history becomes apparent: one would never think it adequate to answer questions on racism in the United States today by responding that a hundred years ago these poor black folks were slaves. Yet this is the effect of dis- missing feminist arguments in the manner of Milton.

Besides, citing aspects of the bitter past does not necessarily de-legitimate the feminist questions. For the ogre of past oppression can be conjured up from two perspectives. On the one hand, it can be used to argue that merely remnants of the past prevent the liberation of women in the new socialist framework. Then one sees structures such as the Chinese street factories as liberating, for they "enable women to engage in the social labor of the community," in the words of Charles Bettleheim, a socialist theoretician.[6] Moreover, the under-representation of women on the revolutionary committees of the factories can be construed as but a leftover from feudalism. On the other hand, references to past oppression can be used to argue quite the reverse: patriarchy, if once so strong and brutal, has surely succeeded in constructing new organizational forms within which to contain women. Then the same structures, the street factories (in which urban wives work while heads of households are more remuneratively employed by the state) are not seen as liberating. Rather, as I argued in the second special issue on women put out by *RRPE*, one notices how these housewives' factories function to reproduce a sexual division of labor, keeping women, as wives, dependent on pooling income with the fathers of their children, in the home.[7]

Footnotes

1. Roxane Witke, "Mao Tse-tung, Women and Suicide," in Marilyn Young, ed. *Women in China,* Michigan Papers on Chinese Studies, No. 15, pp. 7-27.
2. Agnes Smedley, *Portraits of Chinese Women in Revolution,* Feminist Press, Old Westbury, 1975.
3. Ruth Sidel, *Families of Fensheng: Urban Life in China.* Penguin, London, 1974, p. 123.
4. For a Marxian distinction between the dialectical and historicist use of history, see Engels, *Anti-Duhring,* International Publishers, New York, 1972, especially the chapter "Dialectics, Negation of the Negation;" and E.J. Hobsbawn, "Karl Marx's Contribution to Historiography," in *Ideology and Social Science,* Robin Blackburn, ed., Vintage, New York, 1973.
5. Reprinted as an exchange in Young, *op. cit.,* pp. 145-192.
6. Charles Bettleheim, *Cultural Revolution and Industrial Organization in China,* Monthly Review Press, New York, 1974, p. 47.
7. "Women in Transition to Socialism: Perspectives on the Chinese Case," in RRPE, Vol. 8, No. 1, Spring, 1976.

Chapter Ten

The Socialist and Feminist Arguments

Part II: Category of Analysis— Family or Jobs?

Having established the frame of reference, the issue then becomes: what areas should be explored to make the comparison? Socialists look in the general category of work, and tell how women's participation in productive labor has increased. For example, a publication from China, *Ten Great Years,* simply lists the steadily increasing figures of women in the labor force.[1] The feminist argument is critical of this approach for not taking into account the sexual division of labor, either vertical or horizontal. That is, women might go to work outside the home and enter into labor force statistics, but they don't get the top jobs available in industry, such as that of factory administrator; or, women might take part in production, but they are restricted to disadvantaged sectors of the economy, such as small-scale, low-waged street factories set up in neighborhoods for housewives; and even if some women enter traditional male occupations, the flow never seems to be the other way around. As an instance of this last phenomenon, for example, socialist-feminists once on an American delegation to China asked the question: "In our visit to the nursery schools, and in our discussion with some of the people there, we have noticed that the teaching staff is all women. When we asked why this was the case, we were told that this was because women are more suited to this kind of work. We have been told, and we have heard and read before, that one of the major principles in the improvement of the working towards equality of women in China, is that women can do anything men can do. We sense, some of us, a contradiction there. If women can do anything that men can do, cannot men do everything that women can do, and is this seen as a sexual division of labor?" The Chinese women responded by reiterating that the female character just seems to be more suited for the teaching of young children.[2]

Thus confronted, the feminist argument usually turns to examine the family on the assumption that within the family these attitudes about female character are formed. Though understandable, this turn in the argument shortcuts feminist economic analysis or economic analysis of women by saying in effect "well, the socialists look at women's role in the labor force, but that doesn't seem to be adequate, since before women got into the labor force, attitudes about them have been formed. So, we need to examine the family, or non-economic areas. And looking in these other areas, we see that women are still oppressed, since men continue to exercise power over women in the home." Significantly, in the interview previously offered as prototypical of this interaction, the questioning next turned to the area of divorce, which poses the larger theoretical problem of the family's gradual disintegration. "We have read on the procedures for divorce," asked the representative of the American delegation, "that discussion is encouraged between the husband and the wife to try to solve their problems and to avoid the necessity for divorce, and that therefore divorce has decreased in frequency a great deal. The question is, when there is a divorce, what kind of financial arrangements are made and what kind of arrangements are made for the children?" "Divorce is granted only if both parties in the couple desire it," responded the Chinese women. "But divorce is not encouraged, and it used to take a long time—half a year to one year—to do the mediation work, before the divorce is granted. So the organization of both parties would do a lot of work in the mediation, and then it makes an investigation for the granting of the divorce. The organizations and the government try their best to get them reconciled..."

What can we learn from the entirety of this exchange? That socialists and feminists focus on different areas to evaluate the progress of women. The effect would be the same as comparing the color of Israeli grapes to the texture of Egyptian oil, when a truer test would be a close assessment of each country's access to military arms. A step could be taken to re-combine the divergent categories, and alleviate some frustration by saying that "jobs are economic but so is the *household,*" with the household being defined as the economic basis of the social, emotional and psychological relations developed in the family structure.[3] Such a reformulation would allow us to ask: what is the relation between the household and the economy? And what is the relation between women in production and women in the household? Both these relations *together* constitute an analysis of women in the economy. By proposing this analytic merger, I am not rejecting that component of the feminist argument which says "we want to change the family, because given that, women don't get equal access to jobs." On the contrary, I am trying to go one step further by putting the proposal on the economic plane for purposes of equal comparison. To see what the actual significance of the household formation is for women in the economy, I am suggesting that we compare *married women* to *single women*. Thus, at any point in time, we could understand the significance of the existence of the household as a part of the economic structure for women. Another way to get to the bottom would be to break questioning down by age (where are older women in the economy and where are younger women) as age approximates relation to the household. Now we can see the significance of the household in the structure of production as Marx originally did not.

This new framework of analysis connects directly to the line of strategy in the argument of nineteenth century Marxism, which first anticipated a socialistic realization of women's liberation. Insofar as participation in production did not liberate women under capitalism, it was supposed to after the revolution. But not just because the revolution had occurred. More precisely, after the revolution, socialized productivity was to be used to remove the remaining economic functions from the household, and thus the economic basis of the family was to wither away. Now, the socialist argument looks at women's increasing participation in production as if this were an end in itself. Focusing on this category has shifted the lens of socialist analysis away from the disintegration of the family, and hence away from women's liberation. Consequently, when feminists inquire about the state of this process, we are chastized for being "impatient" and "peculiarly American"—and asked to watch as women's liberation gets put off to another historical stage once more. As to the argument about being "peculiarly American," I have shown in a previous section that this has no basis in theoretical history, but I can say more to quell yet another socialist reprimand to a feminist question. The historical fact that a concern developed in one society neither necessarily nor automatically diminishes the relevancy of this concern in the analysis of others. To give but a superficial example, Marx's analysis of the importance of ownership of the means of production is not to be discounted throughout the Third World merely because Marx developed that analytic concern in England.

And in this analysis, new material comes into front-view focus relevant for refining the concept of feminist revolution, as distinct from that defined by using socialist criteria. Let us return to the exchange between the American and Chinese women, by way of illustration. Of particular relevance is the way the younger woman's freedom to participate in production came about at the expense of the older woman "back at the house." In the words of the younger woman interviewed about her overcoming of woman's oppression, "Before liberation, in what we call

the old society, women were subjected to the oppres-
sions of the authority of the political clan, the
religious authorities, the authority of the husband,
the men...Now things have changed...In 1956 I
finished secondary education in my spare time.
Later on, I was trained and became a leading
member of the administration of this factory. Later I
was transferred to work in the County government
in the rural areas.   After 1958 the People's Commune's were established all over the countryside. In
order to build the new countryside, I was transferred
to work in the People's Commune. You know, the
working conditions in the countryside are not as
good as those in the city areas. But I thought of the
past bitter life when the broad masses of working
women were oppressed so I was happy to receive this
task. So I consulted my husband since I wanted to
spend more energy and effort in my work. So my
husband should share the household work with me.
We educated our children to manage their daily lives
with a spirit of self-reliance. I have three children,
and each of them got to know how to manage
housework. For instance, one of them is in charge of
cooking, another in charge of washing, so they have
their division of labor in household work...I have a
mother-in-law. She is 69 years old. She is quite old,
so we advised her to work at home. We also told
her that it is also your support work to manage well
the household work...Thinking of the past life and
contemplating the present good life, I think we
should do more work in our society." Thus the older
woman replaced the younger woman in supervising
the other family members in domestic work, but
housekeeping tasks have remained privatized labor

carried out in the family unit. Realizing that the only shift has been in the age of the responsible woman, we might ask how the oppression of one group of women is expected to liberate another. Strategically, one wonders what will happen when the younger woman gets on in years. Years further into the development process, Soviet grandmothers, who were young girls at the time of the revolution, serve as the organizers of consumption for family members in their daughters' homes.

Footnotes

1. *Ten Great Years.* Statistics of the Economic and Cultural Achievements of the People's Republic of China. Compiled by the State Statistical Bureau, Peking, 1960. This was one of the last compilation documents showing aggregate trends. Since then, China has exhibited a reluctance to release comprehensive data. Even at this point it is interesting to note that the growth rate of females in the labor force was slower than that of males.
2. I am grateful to Bobby Ortiz of Monthly Review for making available to me a transcript of this interview conducted in 1973 on her visit to Shanghai. The women interviewed included a member of the revolutionary committee of a clockshop, a deputy engineer of the Shanghai Physiology Research Institute, a Deputy to the National People's Congress, a woman surgeon, and a staff member of the women's organization.
3. This distinction between the household and the family has since been developed from an anthropological perspective in "The Family as Ideology in the U.S. Class Structure," a paper presented by Rayna Reiter at the Marxist Conference on Social Policy, New School for Social Research, April 30, 1977.

Chapter Eleven

Recombining the Elements: Redefining the Question of Revolution

Let us now take the category of analysis which we have just derived and reapply it to our newly derived frame of comparative reference. Having decided to compare women of different relations to the household to each other, consistency leads us to refine our method of comparing women to men, using the category of relation to the household as well. Thus an expanded category of analysis would be married women/single women to married men/single men. And taking one step further for historical purposes to give us a sense of the dynamics of change, we would arrive at the formulae of married women (then)/ single women (then) to married men (then)/single men (then), and all of this to the same categories *now*. Therefore:

$$\frac{(m♀/s♀: \ m♂/m♂) \ \text{then}}{(m♀/s♀: \ m♂/s♂) \ \text{now}}$$

where m = married

s = single

♀ = women

♂ = men

149

We can expand the framework further by discovering points of incongruency with our inherited categories of analysis. Only the categories of traditional Marxism are relevant here, in this derivation of categories to analyze a socialist case; the actors in the socialist scene went into practice with only these stages of the debate as dress rehearsal. We might draw from our store of knowledge about sex and age differences under capitalism, however, as the problems of capitalism are still those which socialism aims to overcome.

In the beginning, Marx proposed that differences based on sex and age would disappear as members of each group joined the pool of collective labor, assuming the role of individual worker in socialized production. As I have already pointed out, no such entity exists as this "individual worker," since, in forming his method of analysis, Marx abstracted away from differences based on sex and age to analyze the position of the adult male. We have already considerably diversified the point of view, by adding 1) females, and 2) relation to household. We have seen that there are married and single adult males; and married and single adult females. Each of these appears as workers in production; yet in doing so, each is cast in a different role. To concretize with an example, an unmarried woman is likely to get a job different from that of a married man. While the first might become a secretary who is paid barely enough to support herself on the assumption that she shall leave the labor force to marry, the second might become a skilled worker in a plant, or a manager. Either route would place him higher in the hierarchy of work, in terms of skills, but especially in terms of pay. After all, years of struggle have established the assumption that a married man must be paid enough to support not only himself but others. Each of these groups, then, has its own point of view; each sees the economy of life differently.

The household has its own point of view of the economy as well. This often restricts the freedom of its "individual members." For example, a retired working class father may refuse to let his daughter date until she's 25 (as happened to a woman I know in Brooklyn)—thus ensuring that she remains unmarried, that she continues to live at home, that she sacrifices her pay checks to pay the household bills.

Moreover, production has a point of view, as decisions must be made concerning how and when to employ each category of individual worker. "Do we want single women or married women?" the organizers of production must consult among themselves. "Which kind has proven more suitable for the type of work in this factory? Do you remember which type we employed in Taiwan?"

In view of all this, we might ask ourselves a new list of questions. Let's see how the relation to production of all the distinguishable categories of individuals changes over time; how the relation between these different categories of individuals changes; and how the individuals within these categories relate to each other.

Now, how might we categorize the relation between all these groups of different kinds of individuals? They are all "in the household." Yes, but that is too inexact for our purposes, especially as we are interested in how the household changes in relation to production over time. We want to define: 1) the point of view of each category as it faces the household and production; 2) the point of view of the household as it faces production; 3) the point of view of production as it draws these categorized individuals in and out of the household for employment.

We know, of course, that Marx's "individual worker" was really the adult male. This put him in a sex and age group, but not in a relation to the household. Should we view him as a father or as a husband? Should we call the single woman a daughter or a sister? Should we view the single male as a brother or a son? How best to capture for each the differences based on sex and age, differences in relation to the household, and differences in relation to production?

To achieve the goal of such economic characterization, we must move from Marx to Engels. Marx first presumed these differences to be biological, and then proceeded to transcend these differences in his method of analysis, while imagining these differences would eventually decline. Engels, on the other hand, offered an explanation of these differences now, a strategy which he thought would realign them, and an analysis of how they began.

On the perpetuation of differences between men and women that remained under capitalism, Engels' reasoning was: women don't become individuals when they go into production because of the labor the proletarian wife must perform in the home. Her laborious "double duty" exists because of the family. This family arose with private property, as this institution brought with it the necessity for private property owners to control their wives, so that the wives might produce the husbands' heirs. Consequently, the abolishment of private property would remove the economic basis for marriage, allowing for good relations between partners. Hence, women would be liberated.

Even if I am fair to the argument on its own terms, you might observe its failure to approach the dissolution of differences based on sex and age in production. In fact, the only difference Engels examines is that between the adult male and his *proletarian wife*. For two initial reasons, I find this insufficient. First, any woman who is not a wife does not enter into this framework. Second, it only compares differences based on sex within one age group.

I cannot refrain from further pointing out that the strategic goal has changed. While Marx looked toward the *elimination of differences* based on sex and age, Engels turned to look for *better relations* between the adult male and his wife. Abolishing private property may or may not remove the economic basis for marriage; removing the economic basis for marriage may or may not change the marriage relation; but how does even this change counteract the differences based on age and sex in production? Furthermore, what about economic relations between fathers and sons, mothers and daughters, sisters and brothers, fathers and daughters, mothers and sons? How about relations between individuals in these categories and their counterparts or opposites in other households? Do adult males relate only to their wives, or do they also relate to the daughters of other households? Or to their mothers? Do the proletarian wives ever relate to each other? How about the proletarian sons? Do the proletarian sisters ever get together from all the different households, and what happens when they do? How do the relations among all women and among all men change with such an elimination of the material basis for classes?

Finally, shouldn't our goals extend beyond reforming this relation between the adult male and his wife? That is, what if our goal is that the adult male should not claim a wife for himself at all? In other words, Engels' analysis is only good insofar as the household structure itself remains intact, a husband and wife team pooling resources with their common offspring. Under capitalism, we know there have been other alternatives. What might be the economic basis for proceeding with such experimentation?

Of course, it might be unfair to pose all these questions to Engels. So even granting him his one-dimensional approach, where does he take us? Back to the need for owners of property to control their wives as producers of heirs. Let's start from the point of view of the heir, then, to diversify the point of view.

What is an heir? An heir might be called a particular type of offspring, an offspring that receives inheritable wealth from its life-givers. What is an offspring? An offspring might in turn be seen as an age-group sub-category, one that connotes personal ties between "springers" and "sprung." So a generalized category would not be those who bequeath and their heirs, but *producers of offspring* and *offspring*. The force of history makes this higher level of abstraction necessary because private property has been increasingly concentrated in the hands of a few, putting inheritable wealth into a diminishing proportion of wills to be channeled to a shrinking proportion of heirs in the offspring category. But the ties between producers of offspring and offspring remain, although in abstracted form, that of economic dependency of one on the other. One step further along this abstraction moves us from producers of offspring and offspring to *the old* and *the young*. Thus we can derive four categories of individuals at this point, whose form of economic interdependency changes over time with changes in the household, changes in production, and changes occurring throughout the life cycle of the respective individuals. Schematized, they would be:

Producers of Offspring	Offspring
O ♂	Y ♂
O ♀	Y ♀

where O = older
where Y = younger

As we are working towards dynamic rather than static categories, "O" connotes *older* rather than *old*; likewise, "Y" represents *younger* rather than *young*. Neither refers to the literal number of chronological years of an individual. The intent is to progress towards a social category which will allow us to capture the significance of the difference of age within a sex group.

Now, let's move each sex through these two age groups, in search of definite categories. Although each of the four groups relates to production, our goal here is to define them according to the household through which they are economically intertwined. For it is through the household that the "O" feed (or pay for, or give money to, or supply) the "Y" to whom they are personally tied. And vice versa, as when the Y age, they support the O, the latter having a tendency to lose their capacity for economic support of self, let alone for the support of others.

We will assume a point in time in which the household contains a O♂, O♀, Y♂, and Y♀, commonly known as the nuclear household. We know that households, through which these economic transactions occur, change in specific historical conditions. Nonetheless, we aim to define adequate terms for exploring the nature of the changing setting of the transactions first, and to determine the necessary change in the whole system in which these ties and the household formed to mediate them exist.

O♂ :

The standard "individual worker" of Marxism, we could call either a husband or a father. Either would be an advance over the "adult male," since, from this non-relational term, many questionable and irrelevant variables could be loosely inferred as the defining element in his relation to production: physique, mental capacity, "male nature." Even though the designation "adult male" places the "individual worker" in a sex and age category, it does not place him in a relation to the household or in a relation to other household members. Categorizing him as a husband would only capture his relation to individuals of his age group; calling him a father captures his relation across age as well as sex lines. Besides, the distinction characteristic of the O♂ is that he is economically bonded to members of the Y age group.

When he makes this bond (when he fathers children), his relation to production changes, from both his own point of view and from that of the household. He must become a steady earner, increase his earning capacity, and restrict risks he might be tempted to take on the job. For example, he is less likely to experiment, rebel, or change vocations with an increase in the number of dependent mouths to feed at home. Similarly, from the point of view of production, it is assumed that he bears this responsible relation to members of his own age group (the O♀), and to members of the household outside his age group (Y♂ and Y♀). Thus from here on in, our O♂ and Marx's "individual worker" will be known as the *father*.

<u>O♀</u>:

We could characterize the proletarian wife in the Marxist framework as either a wife or a mother. Let us continue to think of her as *wife*, for several reasons. Her distinguishing characteristic is that she forms economic bonds with another member of her age group. Her major change in relation to production occurs when she gets a husband to pay for the members of Y to whom she will be personally tied. Respective of the household protocol which we assumed in time to derive this analysis, she actually produces her offspring only after securing this wife status. Thus *mother* is a sub-category of *wife*. Moreover, while Engels called her a *wife*, he analyzed only her capacity as *mother*: property owners, he explained, oppressed her as producer of personal heirs. As property ownership concentrated in the hands and thus the wills of a few, this capacity of

heir-producer became relevant for a shrinking proportion of wives; yet to Engels, this was still the
rationale for her present existence. Hence we have
inherited a large gap in our analysis of the wife,
which could best be filled by continuing to analyze
her as such.

$\underline{Y_{\female}}$:

The single woman, who was previously non-
existent as an economic individual in analytic categories though not in reality, can be categorized as
either a daughter or a sister. Since we have called her
mother the wife, we will call her the *daughter*. This
continues our emphasis on differences of age within
a sex group. "Sister" is too imprecise; anyone can be
a sister for her whole life, but a daughter is no longer
a daughtor once she becomes a wife, in terms of
primary economic relation to other categories of
individuals. The fact that she is a sister is much less
economically determining compared to the other two
roles. A daughter's primary economic bond is to her
$O_{\male}$ and $O_{\female}$; a wife's primary economic bond is to
someone in her own age group, albeit of the opposite
sex.

$\underline{Y_{\male}}$:

A previously unclassified sub-category of the
"adult male" or "individual worker," the $Y_{\male}$ could
be viewed as a brother or a son. We will call him a
brother, for several reasons. If we call his sister the
daughter, the relation of Y to O is already implied in
our discussion of the Y group as a whole. We need
some way to implicate differences of sex within the Y
itself. Furthermore, we are accustomed to comparing
fathers to sons to see what O holds over Y within the

same sex group, or to see what the latter will get (or take) from the father as he moves on in years. Familiar questions along this line include: did the son take over his father's business? Did the son really deserve to get into the union, or was it through his father? Did the son stay in the class of his father, or, with his father's support or resentment, did he move on? Nevertheless, we are not in the habit of making such comparisons between different sexes within the age group itself. Think, for example, of the expression in American mythology, "the sons of the pioneers moved west." What happened to the pioneers' daughters? Frequently, they worked in mills, sent their wages home, and financed their brothers' big migration. Using the female sex in the younger age group as the exclusive route for tracing cross-generational transactions forces the unequal economic relations of *the daughter* and *her brother* to come into view.

In sum then, with this schema, each sex group contains a member of the Y and the O; each age group contains a member of each sex group. The cumulative result has been:

	♂	♀
O	f	w
Y	b	d

in which f = father
w = wife
d = daughter
b = brother

Both members of the subordinated female sex group have been properly defined in their respective relation to the dominant male (each is daughter and wife of the father). "Mother" would falsely connote strength and power equal to the father; "sister" would wrongly infer equality with the brother. Furthermore, each male character is defined according to his more independent stance ("husband" would mistakenly sound equal to wife; "son" could sound as dependent as daughter, which is false).

Thus we conclude with four categories of individuals, defined from their relation to the household, in their relation to each other. We are now equipped to trace the route of each through production and to distinguish among their variant economic existences. However, we might do this more clearly if we pause for a moment to examine their relation to each other before putting the parts back into the whole. The parts, if you remember, look like this:

$$\text{HH} \left\{ \begin{array}{c} \text{f-w} \\ | \quad | \\ \text{b-d} \end{array} \right. \quad \text{in which HH = household}$$

In the structure of patriarchy, this would more properly be connoted by:

$$\text{HH} \left\{ \begin{array}{c} \overset{f}{\underset{w}{d \nearrow\!\!\uparrow\!\!\searrow b}} \end{array} \right.$$

We could then commence further exploration along the lines of *economic bonds made between f,w,b and d.* This is a generalized category for the historically and class specific "inheritable wealth." The concept implies economic transactions between age groups necessitating a bond between the sexes within the age group (O) that produces the next (Y). The working formula would now be:

$$\frac{\text{w/d : f/b} \quad \text{(then)}}{\text{w/d : f/b} \quad \text{(now)}}$$

From here on in, these will be referred to as *kin catergories*. The advantage in using kin terms over the married/single distinction is that each category of individuals is defined in relation to other categories of individuals, instead of in relation to the structure in which they relate. The advance of kin terms over age distinction is that age *approximates* relation to the household, but is not always its equivalent. For example, where would spinsters and old maids fit into the schema? Equally important is that with these terms we can explore the history of other-than-heterosexuals, who can never legally marry or form households as such. Thus we can examine the economy by means of kin categories, even while the individual household structure is in flux or as it is breaking down.

Finally, with a little bit of imagination, we might be able to conceive of an economic structure which does not rest on the household as we know it today. Both survival and productive resources (income and wealth) might be pooled by all fathers, by all daughters, by all wives, and all brothers—across the general social grouping. This would remove the economic basis of cross-group pooling in the household as such and dissolve the extraordinary power currently held by a sub-group of fathers in the state. If the ties of sex and survival were taken apart, we might envision a means of overcoming alienated sexuality as well as alienated work. This would indeed be a feminist revolution.

"I'll give you four pennies," I said. "I'll take them," he answered, and as I plotted the copper change out all along his counter, I silently said to myself what I had started to say out loud to him: good, then you won't have to pick them up after I throw them at you, like the boys in Indiana threw them at me, back then. Then came a rush of forgotten taunting voices, 'Hey, jew, pick up these pennies!' SPLAT and I saw the little metal coins flinging at me across the playground. 'HEY, jew, we saw you holding hands with Michael in your first date at the carnival!!' THWACK TWUNG and I picked up the gold ones as they slid to the ground from my thigh and I threw them back, trying to keep laughing, wondering, where my girlfriends were at? 'HEY JEW you pregnant? Can't bend down that far? Ha! Whore!!!'

No, actually, this was a memory from childhood, this has nothing to do with the man who was asking me for $2.69 for the pound of cashew nuts he was passing me across the counter of his brighton appetizer store.

No, but actually, this was a memory from childhood, this had nothing to do with what I was wrangling with in my head, trying to order in my head, in my one-room cell they call a bungalow at the Villa on the Coney end of the beach two miles down.

In books about theory-building they say you reach a place where you break out of your cognitive ordering of perception, where you no longer think the correct label for what you had once related to as a moment of passing and to which you now resonate with the feeling of overwhelming significant fact.

165

And where to put it?

That's a state of mind—my whole novel was written like that. For instance, I looked out the window and saw black lines and forgot I was looking at a fire escape.

Artists and writers, they say, in the books about psychoanalysis, resort more often than other people to infantile or primary process thinking. The stress of the mind forces, eventually, an entire reorder. There must be a new synthesis reached after all that splitting. New ways of thinking are developed like that.

I try to keep an image of myself five years ago in focus, as a target for aiming. Sometimes it doesn't work, though. Forgive me for that.

In my journal, I once encouraged myself:

"This is to that dimple-cheeked, long-haired girl with the red bandana and the white teeth and the loving grin, even though she had twice been raped by the age of 20. The girl who wore tall leather boots or perhaps canvas sandles, who had long blue swash-buckling skirts around her knees and sometimes her ankles, and who, on her trip to Latin America, which was an attempt at self-cure, taken out of sheer force to find some meaning for her existence, some reason to keep living, drove past the outskirts of Bogota over mud-soaked roads through the mountains with a government official she met in a fresh coffee cafe— although she refused to be taken to a party. She photographed, and was taken to poetic scenes where the squatters were on the verge of starvation. She rented a jeep of her own and went all by herself to the

166

mines of Zipatatec, where she was shown around by
a scurrying old lady who wanted to show her the
blond headed boy she called a grandson, apparently
fathered by an American when her daughter had
been a maid. She suspected, by the time she got to
Chile, that something was seriously wrong with
more than herself. She even suspected the socialists
were wrong in Chile. And she was right.

"So get to it."

"You want to go on."

"When you explain this to that woman back
then who became tormented with such confusion,
you will, at last, be free. Intellectual self-defense is
just as necessary as the screams in the courtroom of
Inez Garcia."

Taking the ties of sex and survival apart? Was
that really the conclusion of the last chapter?

But the woman in #39 has warned me: it's not
kosher to give away the solution of the plot or the
problems before the end. This advice comes from her
solitary habit of reading mysteries, which she does
alone while the others play cards, get drunk, eat
meals, fling horseshoes or go skinny dipping to-
gether at night in the moonlit ocean. Mysteries, she
assures me, are carefully constructed so as to involve
the reader in guessing solutions. The pursuit of such
engaging activity has addicted her to mysteries for
the last 40 years. I am aware of the fact that I am
writing a completely different sort of book; neverthe-
less I thanked my friendly intelligent neighbor and
retreated from our common verandah into my bright
pink room. Latino radio music zinged out the sound

167

of her advice which I had been respectfully weighing over to myself as I slammed the screen.

So, lest I get ahead of you and the others in this story, let us pause to take stock of where we have come.

We are at the end. The finish. The contours of this shape of the thought have been stretched to the limit.

Perhaps in a new form, after another beginning.

More Titles From South End Press

No Nukes! Everyone's Guide to Nuclear Power
  Anna Gyorgy and Friends
Theatre for the 98%
  Maxine Klein
Ba Ye Zwa The People Live
  Judy Seidman
Unorthodox Marxism
  Michael Albert and Robin Hahnel
Conversations In Maine
  James & Grace Lee Boggs, and Freddy and Lyman Paine
Strike!
  Jeremy Brecher
Between Labor and Capital
  Edited by Pat Walker
The Curious Courtship of Women's Liberation and Socialism
  Batya Weinbaum
Slice the Dreammaker's Throat poetry
  Bill Thompson
U.S. Military Involvement in South Africa
  Edited by Ann Seidman
Creative Differences Profiles of Hollywood Dissidents
  Barbara Zheutlin and David Talbot
European Communism in the Seventies
  Edited by Carl Boggs and David Plotke
Social and Sexual Revolution Essays on Marx and Reich
  Bertell Ollman
Crisis in the Working Class
  John McDermott
Science, Technology and Marxism
  Stanley Aronowitz
Science for the People
  Edited by Rita Arditti, Pat Brennan and Steve Kavrak
What's Wrong with the American Economy?
  Institute for Labor Education
Ecology and Politics
  Andre Gorz
Women and Revolution
  Edited by Lydia Sargent
They Should Have Served That Cup of Coffee
Radicals Remember the Sixties
  Edited by Dick Cluster
The Pentagon-CIA Archipelago
The "Washington Connection" and Third World Fascism
  Noam Chomsky and Ed Herman
Indignant Heart A Black Worker's Journal
  Charles Denby (Matthew Ward)

Our full catalogue and information about becoming a South End
Press book member are available on request.
South End Press, P.O. Box 68, Astor Station
Boston, Mass. 02123 tel. (617) 266-0629